Dog Trair
and Behaviour Sc

Contributors: Sally Bradbury
Emma Judson
Vidhyalakshmi Karthikeyan
Claire Martin
Rebecca Köhnke
Jo Maisey
Kay Bradnum
Abby Huxtable
Kate Harland
Leah Roberts
Wagging Wonders Lincoln
Daisy Moore

Illustrated by Emma Judson

Designed and Edited by Jo Maisey & Anna Bentz

Preface

How the Book Came About

Back in the early days of Facebook groups, several dog trainers and behaviour geeks 'met' online through their common interest in force-free, fear-free training and behaviour modification techniques.

They created the Facebook group *Dog Training Advice and Support (DTAS)* in 2012 to ensure that people looking for advice and help on dog training and behaviour matters on Facebook received safe, practical advice, based in modern science. Although social media is not necessarily the ideal place to look for such information, it's often where people turn to as a first port of call. They wanted to ensure that people were pointed in the right direction.

The group has gone from strength to strength and is widely recommended by breeders, vets and other professional trainers and behaviourists.

The articles in this book are taken from the guides in the group and are a culmination of responses to behaviour and training questions from group members. You will notice that we use the word 'cue' rather than 'command'. We also prefer to 'teach' rather than 'train'. The preferred use of these words may seem like a small thing, but it can affect how we perceive our relationship with our dog.

Brought to you by the professional team behind DTAS.

Contents

Chapter 1   **First, Do No Harm** **1**

The Dangers of Aversives 2

The Difference Between 'No' and Other Words 8

Chapter 2   **Puppies** **11**

Two Puppies? Littermate Syndrome 12

Introducing a New Puppy to the Family Dog(s) 18

Puppies and Time 19

Puppy's First Night 21

Cry It Out? 22

Raising a Puppy 25

Toilet Training 27

Puppy Biting 30

Puppy Biting and Play 32

Games to Play with Your Puppy 34

Socialising: The Good, The Bad and The Consequences 34

Socialising and Social Distancing 37

Crate Training 37

The Lounge is for Lounging 47

Puppy's First Walk 47

Happy Puppy Care 49

Four on the Floor – Preventing Jumping Up 50

Zoomies 51

Puppy Confidence 53

Fear Periods 57

Chapter 3   **Separation Anxiety or Frustration** **61**

Preventing Separation-Related Anxiety or Frustration 62

Getting Puppy or New Dog Used to Being Alone 67

Doorway to… Enlightenment? 78

Chapter 4   **Anxious and Fearful Dogs** **81**

Calming Products and Anxiety Medications 82

Working with Fear Issues 83

My Puppy is a Scaredy Cat 84

Trigger Stacking 85

Reactive Dogs 87

Reactive Dog Myths 91

Noise Phobias and Fireworks 92

Fireworks Season and Dogs 94

Fear of Car or Travel 96

Afraid of Visitors 97

Chapter 5   Recall 99

Teaching Recall 100
Choosing and Using a Long line 103
Prey Drive 105

Chapter 6   Resource Guarding 107

Resource Guarding: Normal or Not? 108
Prevention of Resource Guarding 111
Food Aggression and Jess 112
Resource Guarding Owner 115

Chapter 7   Loose Lead Walking (LLW) 117

General Advice before you Start 118
Loose Lead Walking 118
Teaching a Dog to Walk on a Lead 122

Chapter 8   Barking 123

Reasons for Excessive Barking 124
Prevention of Unwanted Barking 127

Chapter 9   Dogs and Babies 131

Preparing your Dog for the Arrival of a Baby ... 132
Pram Training 137

Chapter 10   The Multi-Pet Household 141

Living in a Multi-Dog Household 142
One Dog Good. Seven Dogs Better? 145
Bringing Home a New Dog 148
Cats and Small Furries 152

Chapter 11   Unwanted Behaviours 155

Undesirable Behaviours 156
My Dog Doesn't Listen to Me 158
Reacting to Kissing and Cuddling 160
Things that Go Bump in the Night 161
Poo Eating (Coprophagia) 162
Frustrated Greeter 164
Jumping in Excitement at Visitors 165
Counter Surfing 166
Door Dashing 166
Chasing and Lunging at Cars 167
Begging 167
Digging 168
Shadow or Light Chasing 168

Chapter 12 Skills for a Happy Life **169**

Where do I Start? What Should my Dog Know? 170

Exercising Your Dog's Mind 171

Teaching Self-Control 173

Teaching a Down 174

Desensitising to Car Journeys 175

Road to Nowhere 176

Moving To a New House 177

Muzzle Love 178

Chapter 1

First, Do No Harm

WHEEL
OF
FALL-OUT

The Dangers of Aversives
The use of aversives to stop unwanted behaviour
By Emma Judson

You've probably heard the words 'punishment', 'correction', and maybe even 'aversive', but what do they actually mean?

Science defines 'positive punishment' as something you do to your dog that they find unpleasant (painful or scary, for example), which results in the reduction in frequency of that behaviour.

An aversive is something your dog doesn't like; something he would like to avoid having happen again. If your dog pairs an action, behaviour, or event, with an aversive, there is a chance he will avoid that situation or that action in future.

The terms 'correction' and 'punishment' can be misleading. People use them incorrectly or don't understand what they mean. For example, some people think a correction is fine and a punishment is horrid. It all boils down to this – if you do something to your dog and he does not like it and would like to avoid it happening again, then that is aversive. If it serves to reduce the frequency of a behaviour, then it is a punishment. It doesn't matter what you call it, or what your intentions were; if it's aversive, and it makes your dog think twice about performing that behaviour, then that is what it is. I have yet to find anyone using the word 'correction' who is actually telling the dog what the correct thing is. They're delivering an aversive every time.

However, and here we come back to that scientific definition of a punishment, it needs to reduce the frequency of a behaviour. If it doesn't, or if it did and then it stops working but you continue doing it, it is no longer a punishment. It may, however, still be unpleasant for your dog!

What would you call something unpleasant, painful, or scary that someone keeps doing to you even though it isn't improving your behaviour? I'd call it abusive.

And even if the aversive is altering behaviour, that's still not ok. That is still a problem. To understand the reason for this, we first need to look at human behaviour. The principles of learning theory apply to us as well as dogs. If we do something that works or that is rewarding to us, we do it again. That's positive reinforcement. So, Dave jerks Fido's lead to stop him from pulling when walking, Fido stops pulling for a bit, Dave thinks, 'well that worked', and he has been positively reinforced for delivering an aversive to Fido.

Let's say that this works as far as Dave is concerned for a week. At the end of the week, however, Fido sees a squirrel disappear over a wall and so he pulls, and this time, when Dave jerks, Fido doesn't stop pulling. What does Dave do now? Well, he's always been rewarded for jerking Fido's lead, so the logical thing for Dave to do is jerk the lead harder!

Now, if you're saying 'no, no, Dave would think of something else, surely', let me ask you this:

- What do you do if your pen stops writing? Get out a new one or scribble a bit harder?
- What do you do if the key won't turn in the lock? Call a locksmith immediately or shove the key in and out, wiggle it a bit harder, and rattle the handle a bit?
- What do you do if the kids upstairs don't hear you yell them down for tea? Go upstairs or yell a little louder?

Be honest, we all experience this. It's called an extinction burst. If a behaviour we've previously been rewarded for stops being rewarding, we will try harder and harder before we eventually admit defeat.

So, Dave jerks Fido's lead harder, and it hurts Fido, and he squeaks and walks nicely for a bit. Now that Dave has been rewarded for jerking harder, he's more likely to do it again.

But Fido's neck is becoming thick with extra muscle, and the nerve endings are deadening as a result of all this tugging and jerking. So, when Fido pulls even harder, and Dave jerks harder, and Fido doesn't respond... Now what?

Well, there's a strong chance Dave will use two hands and yank Fido off his feet, but he might also look at something like a prong collar or even a shock collar. Why? Because he thinks he needs something stronger to get Fido to listen to him.

Once you've started working your way up that scale of aversives, it is very difficult to stop. There are risks involved beyond 'just' increasing the aversiveness:

- **Pain.** It hurts, that is why it works
- **Fear.** It's scary, that might also be why it works
- **Physical damage.** Many aversives are designed to cause pain, and with pain comes damage; collapsed tracheas, bruised necks, burnt skin, damaged joints, the list goes on
- **Mental damage.** Subjecting anyone to aversive experiences they cannot escape from will cause psychological damage. Sometimes, just a one-off experience will have a negative effect. Other times, the damage occurs after repeatedly using the aversive. In humans, we'd call this post-traumatic stress disorder (PTSD). There is no guaranteed cure for PTSD in humans. There is scientific evidence on the effects of prolonged stress and repeated trauma on dog behaviour. If we can't fix PTSD in humans who can talk to us, what chance do we have in dogs?
- **Incorrect associations.** This is where the dog links the aversive with something other than his own behaviour
- Worsening or new **behavioural problems** due to the suppression of behaviour

Using aversives does not treat the underlying cause of the problem. The behaviour you are seeing is a symptom of a physical or emotional state or condition, or it is just something dogs do that is inconvenient for people. Simply stopping that behaviour is not addressing the cause of that behaviour.

Let's go back to Fido and Dave. Fido naturally moves faster than Dave. His natural and preferred pace for a walk would actually be a trot, around 5 -7 mph. Dave's preferred pace is a leisurely walk of around 2.5 mph. If you've ever tried to halve your walking pace to match a child or elderly relative, you will understand why Fido struggles.

So, to begin with, we need to teach Fido to walk slowly without pulling. He doesn't know how to do this. It isn't natural for him. We need to give Fido a reason to walk with a person. Instead of teaching him 'it is painful if you go ahead of the person and pull', we could teach him 'it's really rewarding to look at the person and stick next to them'. We can simply drop treats down on the floor as we walk.

But Dave has gone for the aversive, so what happens next?

Since Fido is wearing a collar, all those lead jerks are happening around his throat. Dave asks someone in the pub about this, and they show him a thin slip lead that is placed high up on the dog's neck behind the ears. This, Dave is told, is the 'proper' way to use a slip lead. It's more effective this way. The person telling Dave this is an ex-police dog trainer, and they are not wrong, but they haven't explained why. It is more effective because a thin slip lead, rather than Fido's broad collar, coupled with the placement high up behind the ears and under the throat, will cause Fido more pain when he pulls or when Dave jerks the lead.

So, Dave tries this out. He gives it a go on a Saturday morning walking through town.

First, they meet Mrs Bunn the Baker. Fido pulls forwards to say 'Hi'. He likes Mrs Bunn… JERK! OUCH!

Then they meet Mr Bones the Butcher. Fido pulls forward to say 'Hi'. He really likes Mr Bones… JERK, OUCH!!!

Then they meet Mr Smith the Fishmonger (what?!). Fido pulls forward to say 'Hi'. He really likes stinky Mr Smith… JERK! OUCHHHH!!!!!

Then they meet Little Jimmy the Loveable Child. Fido pulls forward and then… Growls at Little Jimmy, bares his teeth, barks loudly and backs off… And gets a jerk and slap on the nose for growling and making Little Jimmy cry!

What happened here? Well, Fido wasn't really aware that he was pulling on the lead to greet people. He was focused solely on the people – his favourite people! He was only thinking of people each time he got a painful jerk to the neck. So, when he met Little Jimmy, he associated seeing a favourite person with feeling pain. He did what a dog does when a situation occurs that he feels worried or threatened by. He growled, bared his teeth, and barked to get Little Jimmy to back off… And he still got a jerk in the neck and a slap on the nose.

Now he has learned that people are bad news, whether you approach or not! He may also have learned that warning people about how you feel (by growling) is a bad idea, because that earned him more pain.

The following week, Dave takes Fido into town to do the shopping. It's Fido's first walk since he growled at Little Jimmy as Dave has been too busy. He is quite pleased as Fido seems to be sticking closely to him today, not leaving his side. The training must be working!

Here comes Little Jimmy! He's sneaking up behind Dave and Fido as they wait at the bus stop. He's going to surprise them by jumping out in front of them to say 'Hi'. He's totally forgotten about Fido growling and barking at him last week because he's 10 and this is a story.

Little Jimmy jumps out, 'HI! SURPRISE!'

Fido is shocked! Here is the person that meant a jerk and a slap last week! He knows he can't growl; it will get him a slap. He can't back up either as they're standing against a wall, and he can't run as he is on the lead. So, as Little Jimmy bends down to pat Fido's head, Fido snaps and catches Little Jimmy's hand with his teeth… Oh dear, Fido. Oh dear.

While this story is fiction, it is based entirely on real events. Fido is an amalgamation of several dogs I have been called on to help, and who had bitten people as a result of using aversives and positive punishment.

There are lots of aversive devices and training techniques out there, and I can't possibly list them all. There are collars and harnesses designed to tighten and choke or squeeze a dog's sensitive areas. There are collars designed to really hurt, with prongs on the inside or electrodes to shock. Some are intentionally mislabelled as delivering a 'tap', a 'stimulation', or a 'buzz', but if it's got electrodes, it's giving a shock. There are slip leads, and even braces to hold them up over the sensitive structures behind the ears.

With some of them, it's obvious that they are designed to be aversive. Some are more subtle, because when it comes down to it, it is the dog who decides what he or she finds aversive – not you, and not me. So, your dog may hate water being sprayed in her face and my dog might love it. It is an aversive for your dog, and a reward for mine.

Some aversives may look innocuous, like a can of pebbles or pennies, a ribbon loop with metal discs, or a bunch of keys or a chain. When thrown down on the ground, these all make a startling sound. They might not ever touch the dog, but startling someone to stop their behaviour is unkind, ineffective, and can have negative effects, such as sound phobias, which are very hard to fix.

Some aversives are awful on a psychological level, which can be every bit as damaging as the physical punishments.

The most horrific thing about aversives is that they don't need to be used at all! Dogs, like Fido, experienced them unnecessarily. There are ways of teaching that could have been fun and enjoyable for Fido!

If Fido had been put on a harness, so that pulling never hurt him, he would have had a very different experience. If he had been taught using rewards, and even more rewards when Little Jimmy or Mr Bunn appeared, so that he understood staying next to Dave was a good thing, then he would almost certainly have bounced back from his startle at Little Jimmy jumping out in surprise. He would have been happy to see Little Jimmy the Loveable Child. He wouldn't have been worried that he couldn't run and couldn't growl as he would not have needed to!

Next time someone suggests a training method or device to you, ask them (and yourself) these questions:

- How does this work?
- What does my dog get if he gets it right?
- What are the risks?
- Why is the behaviour occurring in the first place?
- What could I teach instead of the unwanted behaviour?

Thinking about these things will help you decide whether you should follow the method. In case you need a bit more help, my final rules of thumb are these:

- If it starts with 'this sounds awful but', then it is awful. Don't do it
- If it starts with 'you have to be cruel to be kind', then it is cruel, and no you don't. So, don't do it
- If it would get you locked up (rather than, say, raised eyebrows) if you applied the method to a toddler, then don't do it!

The Difference Between 'No' and Other Words

By Daisy Moore

Yesterday, I saw a comment on a thread, which got me thinking. Many people know that dogs don't speak our language, and so the only meaning of words is what we condition the word to mean. Many people are also aware that the use of the word 'no' is sometimes controversial. And sometimes, people say that 'no' means nothing to the dog. So, does that mean that we can teach a dog what 'no' means by conditioning it to mean something?

The problem here is what 'no' means to us humans. We use 'no' to mean 'stop that'. And 'stop that' is actually really vague. I'm going to go off into a weird analogy here, but please bear with me.

You are in someone's house; you don't speak their language and they don't speak yours. You are in their living room, sitting on the couch, drinking a cup of tea. They say 'wibble' to you, in a neutral tone of voice. You have no idea what 'wibble' means. You continue. They say 'wibble' to you in a harsh tone of voice with a displeased look on their face. OK, so you can use your rational, human brain to realise that they might not be happy about something. It might be totally unrelated to you, but let's not overcomplicate things. They shout 'wibble', and you get off the sofa, put the cup of tea down, and get away from them. They stop shouting.

You have learnt (by being intimidated) that 'wibble' means they aren't happy about something you're doing, but you don't know what!

Next time you're in this room, you see a cup of tea near the sofa. You think, 'OK the tea isn't for me, I won't touch it'. But the person still says 'wibble' at you. They don't need to shout, now. You have worked out they aren't pleased, and you want to avoid being shouted at again. But why are they saying 'wibble'? You didn't touch the tea. The person continues to say 'wibble', getting a little angry at your defiance. What on earth do they want? Eventually you decide just to get off the sofa and out of the room. The person looks pleased.

Next time you're in this room, you decide to avoid the tea and the sofa. But you're getting told 'wibble' again! Argh! What do they want????

There are two points to this long story:

1. How do you attach meaning to the word? If I say 'wibble' at you with a neutral tone and neutral face, you have no idea that it means that I

don't like what you're doing, and I want you to stop. So, to attach that meaning, the person in the story shouted. So, how would you attach the 'stop that' meaning to the word 'wibble'?

2. Using words like 'no' to mean 'stop that', doesn't tell the dog what you **do** want them to do. The person in my story doesn't have any idea why they're being told 'wibble'. They don't mean to do the wrong thing, but they can't work out what to do. They're also frustrated, because they're trying to do the right thing but keep getting it wrong, and there's no guidance. The person saying 'wibble' is also frustrated because their guest keeps doing the wrong thing, even though they've been told not to!

The 'wibble' person doesn't mind you on the sofa, and they actually made the tea for you. They just don't like shoes on their rug. But how could you work that out with the information you were given?

The word 'no' isn't an inherently bad thing. We are all human, so we tend to use words like humans do. Saying 'no' doesn't make you a bad person! But if you're using it to try to change your dog's behaviour, there may be a much more efficient way to do that, which will be more enjoyable for you both! What do you want the dog to do instead?

The problem with 'no' isn't the word itself, it's how we use it. It's the meaning that we attach to the word, how we do it, and how confusing it becomes when we say 'no' in so many different situations.

Chapter 2

Puppies

Two Puppies? Littermate Syndrome
Raising Littermates
By Sally Bradbury

If you are considering buying two puppies together or if you already have a puppy and are considering getting another, please read this first.

Littermate Syndrome (LMS) is a collection of symptoms that can occur together when two littermates or two puppies of similar age are raised in the same home. Precautions must be taken to minimise or prevent these symptoms from occurring.

Where one puppy would be bonding with his new human at 8–12 weeks old, two puppies that stay together are continuing to bond with each other, to the exclusion of the new person in their lives.

Ensuring that each pup develops separately would require two dedicated people to take a puppy each and give them the attention and bonding opportunities that a single pup would have.

This means that in the early days, each pup spends ALL of their time with a person and only a limited amount of time with the other pup.

This includes:

- Co-sleeping with their person
- Separate walks
- Separate play
- Separate training
- Separate meals

It is recommended to walk and play with the pups separately during this bonding period. Occasionally walk and play together so that both pups learn to be attentive to their person with the distraction of each other.

I have two pairs of siblings. The **only** reason we got two puppies at the same time from the same litter is that we both wanted a pup from that litter. (We compete in agility.) Three years later, the same happened again.

In order to prevent problems associated with LMS, we made sacrifices and put in a lot of work.

First of all, we collected one puppy from the breeder and left the other one for six days so that they were totally separated for that time.

When we brought the second puppy home, another week passed before they met again.

Hubby and I slept separately with a puppy each. The pups didn't see each other during night-time toilet trips and early mornings. Nor did we.

Both of us spent lots of time training, playing, and bonding with our pup. Then both of us spent lots of time training, playing, and bonding with them both. So everything they could do individually, they could also do together, without being distracted by each other.

Mostly, they were walked separately up to about nine months old.

I usually recommend this sort of separation for up to a year to ensure that you have two separate dogs responding to you when you do walk them together. Not two halves of a whole.

I have seen many heart-breaking cases of LMS in my professional career. I have helped with re-homing a fair few halves of pairs as well, with ages ranging between eight weeks and 18 months.

Problems I have seen include:

- Dogs that scream when they are apart and fight when together
- Pairs that are totally oblivious to their humans. One pair even ran into their owner when they were playing and broke her leg
- Others, where one pup has developed normally and the other is dysfunctional

Once this has developed, it is very difficult to turn it around because some things can only be learned in puppyhood. The dogs need to be separated to have any chance at rehab, but often one or both simply cannot function without the other one so it's a Catch 22.

Obviously, even though I've done it, I don't recommend it unless there are two dedicated and experienced adults that are going to raise them.

Double Trouble – Two Puppies at Once?
By Emma Judson

Hopefully you are reading this *before* buying any puppies at all and are only considering having two puppies at the same time, possibly littermates.

STOP! Sit back down. Hold your horses. Wait a second.

Raising two puppies at once is one of those things that one or two people, someone you've heard of, maybe a family member, did and got lucky. We will come back to these people later!

Believe me, for the rest of you, it's a slippery slope to a *nightmare* and a catastrophe and a wholly unenjoyable puppy/dog owning experience.

First, ask yourself why two puppies seem a better idea than one puppy?

The top answer is because 'two will keep each other company'. Now, ask yourself why you need them to keep each other company? Would that be because you aren't going to be there so much?

If the answer is yes, then honestly, you don't have the time for one puppy. Not without making some other arrangements such as a puppysitter, a doggy daycare or crèche, a family member minding the pup during the day, or being able to take the puppy into work with you.

If none of the above can be done, then either wait until it can, or consider an older dog who can cope with being left. Dog ownership is a privilege for those who have the time, money, and patience. Not a right for those who plain 'want'.

Next top answers will be 'because they are cute/because the kids wanted one each/because we couldn't split them up/because we couldn't choose between them/because the breeder offered us a discount if we took two'.

Puppies only *look* cute because if they didn't, we wouldn't put up with the horrible things they do. Puppies are *not* really cute at all. Stop thinking about cute. It baffles your brain, and you forget the important things in life. Cute is a survival mechanism. It's there to trick you. Ignore it! Puppies are incontinent, puppies *bite*, and they bite *hard*. Puppies make extremely loud noises and demand and *need* your attention 24 hours a day. Puppies are extremely expensive, tiring and will eat your most expensive stuff, rip up your carpets and sofa, and drag your shoes out into the yard to bury them. They make the neighbours hate you. Make you sleep deprived. Make you stand in poo or wee. Puppies are not cute!

What kids want, while sometimes important, is *not* important when it comes to 'I want a puppy'. Yes, sure they want a puppy. Next week, they will want to swap it for a games console. The week after, they want a skateboard. I have nothing against kids. I was one. But what kids want when it comes to cutesy things is *not* a reason to commit to 12+ years of dog ownership.

Splitting puppies up is *good* for them. If they are together, puppies only practise being puppies, and I will get on to what that really means in a moment. Puppies do *not* learn how to be nice sensible adult dogs from other puppies, just like toddlers do not learn how to be quantum physicists from other toddlers. They learn this from adults.

In any given 'wild' situation, baby animals of sociable species split up as they hit adolescence. Between 'baby animal' stage and 'adolescent' stage, they mix with a *wide* range of other ages of animal of their species. From similar aged animals to old ones, and from nice ones to crabby ones, and everything in between. When everyone in their social group is fed up with them, they go on their merry way to seek their fortunes in the big, wide world. Occasionally, some buddy up for a while through choice. A choice made as adolescents and adults.

In your home, there is no choice. They are stuck there. Permanently. In a tiny space. Those pups have grown up only with each other, rather than with other adult dogs, aunties, uncles, and cousins, who would have taught them all manner of things. Who is to say whether they will still love each other through adolescence and choose to stick together, or whether they will hate one another with a vengeance and fight to the death? Certainly not you or me. And do you *want* to live with the possibility that this will happen, and you will have to choose between your beloved pets? Or live with the fear that, one day, someone will leave a door open and Fluffy will rip Precious' head off? Or that King and Prince will fight, and your toddler will get in the middle of it and get hurt?

Believe me, splitting up puppies at eight weeks is as easy as anything compared with the horror of discovering one of your dogs wants to kill the other.

If you can't choose, toss a coin, let the breeder choose, or go for a walk and think about it for a little while longer. You will find a way of choosing.

You have made harder choices before in your life and you will probably come across harder ones again in the future.

And finally – because the breeder offered you a discount?

Any breeder who is happy to sell people two puppies from the same litter, *especially* same sex littermates, has only one thing on their mind. Your money.

They don't care if the puppies live happily ever after. They don't care if you spend the next 12 years in a living hell. They don't care if you have to take one to the vet to be put down. They just want your money.

The same goes for puppy farms, pet stores and backyard breeders. Along with the breeders of wolf x or made-up breeds, all who breed or sell pups without the health tests necessary, without care or consideration towards the parent dogs, without giving you the advice you need to make sure your pup lives a long and happy life; they are in it for the cash and nothing more.

So, you don't want two puppies to keep each other company because you reckon you have the time. You aren't doing it just because they are cute, and you reckon the breeder is a responsible and reputable kind of person.

You still shouldn't get two puppies.

They will take three times the work of one, if not more. Everything you do with one puppy, you must do separately with the other puppy and again, together with both.

So, that's three times the socialisation, three times the training, and three times the walkies.

It's also a million times harder to toilet train two pups, because if you have them outdoors together, they will play and forget to poop. Put one indoors while you do the other, the one indoors messes in the house.

Unless there are *two* adults fully committed to doing this work in the same way as one another or you have achieved omnipresence, it's going to take way longer.

How many months of wee and poo on your floors are you going to be happy with? Because realistically, one puppy takes up to nine months to be reliably house trained. With two, you could easily have 18-month-old, almost adult dogs still going in the house or whenever your back is turned.

So, you need two adults to train them together. You can't leave them alone together because if you think one puppy can cause some destruction when left alone, you haven't seen a *thing* compared to what two puppies can do. Eat your sofa? Rip up your carpets? Or put them outdoors and watch them eat through the neighbour's fence and howl and play fight all day long.

And that is when they still like one another. Wait until they reach sexual maturity and decide that this town ain't big enough for the both of them.

As I said at the beginning, there's always going to be someone you know, or you heard of, who reckons they made it work. I'd say for every one of those people who is actually telling the truth, ten more are lying or at least glossing over some details. Ask more detailed questions. Ask them where they can and cannot take their dogs. You'll find out most likely that their dogs never leave the property or cannot be separated because one yells the house down if the other leaves the building. Or they can't be kept together because one wants to kill the other. Or they can't be trusted around guests. Or they won't walk nicely on the lead. Or, or, or.

Question these folks who say it's OK and find out if their lifestyle is actually anything like yours. Maybe it did work for them. I'm not saying it never can, but there's a degree of luck there. And maybe you find out that this person is home all day, has ten acres of well-fenced land, and no neighbours for 100 miles in any direction. Maybe they show dogs or work them. There will be some details that mean what works for them may well *not* work out for you.

Most people make mistakes with puppies. We are only human after all, and mistakes are something we humans do pretty well. One undersocialised puppy is a pain to deal with. Two are a nightmare. By the time you realise that two puppies were a mistake, it's usually going to be one of those pups who suffers for your error the most.

If you have already got two puppies, you might think I am over-reacting or painting a very bleak picture to scare you. Believe me I am not writing this to wee on anyone's parade. We all have dogs because we like them, and we have a vision in our heads of what our life with our adult dog is going to be like. It's going to be fun and fairly carefree with our dog by our side, obeying our cues, and having a ball.

By taking on two puppies at once, you drastically reduce the chances of that becoming a reality. You only need to take a look in rescue centres and shelters around the world to see that *millions* of people fail to raise *one* dog every single day.

Why make it any harder than it already is? The world is rapidly becoming less and less dog-friendly and dogs are expected to behave impeccably in every situation. Give yourself the very *best* chance you *and* your dog can have of having a happy life together. Get *one* pup at a time from a reputable shelter or breeder. If you got two pups together and you are struggling with them now, **TAKE ONE BACK**. Re-home him or her. It's a lot easier to do now at a few weeks old than it will be in 6- or 12-months' time when it's not just a struggle. Very few people want to take on half-grown out of control pups who have learned bad habits from their sibling.

Introducing a New Puppy to the Family Dog(s)
By Sally Bradbury

Introducing a puppy to the existing dog(s) needs to be done slowly and carefully, while ensuring that they both get lots of one-to-one attention and that the puppy is not allowed to be a nuisance to the older dog. First impressions and experiences are going to shape their future relationship.

A lot will depend on how sociable the current dog is and his/her experience with puppies. Some dogs just don't do puppies. Occasionally, an adult dog may be scared of a puppy.

Use stair gates in doorways or a puppy pen so that they can see each other without interacting. Then you can be guided by how they react to each other. If you have more than one dog, then they should meet the puppy one at a time initially.

The initial introductions may be successfully accomplished the first day puppy comes home, or it may take longer. It pays to take all the time you need to ensure that nothing goes wrong.

Contrary to popular belief, it is not advantageous to have the adult dog 'tell the puppy off'. It's not fair on either of them. There are very few suitable teaching dogs and those that are, are able to teach and guide puppies without using their teeth and frightening the puppy.

A new puppy needs to spend 24/7 with his humans in the early days and limited, supervised time with the other dog(s).

Always feed dogs separately and apply the same rule to chew toys or indeed anything that either dog may not want to share.

Puppies and Time
Or NO, you REALLY can't leave your puppy alone

By Emma Judson

For some reason, many people expect that a puppy can be left alone for an hour, two hours, sometimes significantly longer than that, after the first day or so. Some people are more realistic. They think that it's going to be OK after the first week or two. The horrible, harsh reality is this – at eight weeks old, a puppy requires your attention about as much as an eight-week-old human baby would. It may be *legal* to leave your eight-week-old puppy for two hours while you do your Friday Big Shop, but it is as dangerous and as damaging to him as it would be to the human baby of the same age. Your puppy needs his primary caregiver's supervision constantly – and since you took him away from Mum, that's you.

If you want to raise a dog who is well behaved, has a normal temperament, is not predisposed to behavioural issues, such as separation anxiety, ingrained toilet training issues, or general anxiety, then this is as important as teaching him to sit or lie down, or feeding him the right food every day. What might happen if you leave a pup for just an hour and he can't handle it? He might experience severe distress, fear that his world has just ended, and the sense that he will never be safe and secure again; the sort of fear that makes him urinate and defecate uncontrollably. That's what is happening when you leave a pup and they are screaming for you to come back, messing in the house or their bed or your kitchen floor, shredding the doorways, or lifting the carpet. That's upsetting for you, it's expensive, as well, and will probably get you in trouble with your neighbours or even the environmental health department, if the noise is too much.

But what about your puppy? What's that doing to his developing brain? People will commonly tell you that 'he'll get over it', or 'he will quiet down eventually', or 'he needs to get used to it'. He won't. He might collapse and sleep through sheer exhaustion or shut down mentally. And while yes, they do need to get used to being left, the way to do it is not to just *leave* him without any warning or preparation. The grim reality is that this severe distress is likely to negatively affect his brain development, predisposing him to being anxious, fearful, and sensitive to noises and movement. It is likely to negatively affect his ability to communicate well with other dogs, his ability to tolerate normal day to day stress and his ability to learn. All of which means he is less well equipped and less likely to be that steady companion dog you wanted. (And if you wanted a bundle of nerves and fear with behaviour problems, go ask any rescue for one, they will all be able to help you out there.)

What else can happen? Well, your pup could injure themselves badly. I know of one pup who broke his leg so severely at nine weeks when left alone for just 20 minutes that he had to have it amputated before he was 14 weeks old. He is also *terrified* of being left alone now, quite understandably. I have heard of pups getting stuck, caught by collars or just by their jaws, and suffocating, and pups who have fallen off or pulled furniture over and been severely injured or crushed to death.

But I Want a Puppy and I Work

Well, just because 'you want', doesn't mean 'you should have', does it? I know that's hard to hear; it's not what *anyone* wants to hear, but we are all adults. We should know that sometimes, what we want is not what we can have. Sometimes, someone else's needs and welfare will come before our own. That said, there are ways around it if you are willing to make compromises.

- Hire a dog-sitter
- Find a quality dog daycare
- Consider taking on an older dog who is OK with being left
- Change your employment for a job where you work from home
- Go self-employed in a job where your dog can come too
- Change shift patterns so there is always someone home
- Take a long (six month) sabbatical so you can help your puppy settle in

Regardless of which option you decide to take, factor in at *least* two weeks to get a pup settled in and ideally a month. This may well mean two adults taking all their annual leave as two fortnights, one after the other. NOTE: this does not mean 'two weeks before you can leave the puppy for hours on end'. It means 'two weeks where you will do nothing but deal with the puppy'.

But, But, But!

… my friend/neighbour/relative had a puppy and they left their's 1/2/3/4/5/6/7/8 hours a day from day one and it was <u>fine</u>!

Really? Was it really fine? Do they live somewhere remote or with thick walls so that the neighbours cannot hear the puppy? Did they put the puppy outdoors in a kennel to stop it wrecking the house? Is that dog a superb, well-balanced easy-going dog that is well trained and can go anywhere and do anything? If it is, that is lucky and rare. I can show you many thousands of dogs handed into rescues at eight or nine months old, because their owners tried this and were sick of the stress, the mess, and the complaints. Of course, the dog is now adolescent, doesn't listen and is so stroppy that they have had enough. In most cases, if their owners had simply taken the time needed or waited until they had the time before getting a puppy at all, then the pups would not have landed in rescue. For every dog that 'it worked' for, I'll show you a hundred it didn't work for at all. That's the truth, as unpleasant as it is.

But my Puppy is Fine when Left

Again, is he really? And how is his house-training? And does he chew on stuff? Does he like being crated or shut in the kitchen? How's he doing at puppy class or training classes? Is he at the same stage as other dogs his age? Because all that time a puppy spends *without* you is time spent not only NOT learning how to be a nice, easy-to-live-with, adult dog, but also learning all the things you *don't* want him to do. If you aren't supervising, house training takes longer. Basic training takes longer. Forming a strong bond of trust takes longer. When you are not supervising, your puppy is learning to poo and pee where *he* likes, to chew what he wants, to bark at sounds he hears, to rip up your carpet and sofa cushions, shred his bedding inside his crate, or chew the crate bars. And that is, of course, even if he is genuinely fine. Many dogs are *not* fine at all; they just don't display obvious symptoms like barking, crying or destroying things.

In Conclusion

I am certain that people reading this will be feeling upset and think that what I am saying is unfair. The reality is that this is written so that people do not make mistakes that lead to dogs suffering and end up being sold on or in rescue. You presumably want a dog because you love dogs. You want to enjoy dog ownership and have a happy, friendly dog who has a lovely life. Getting a puppy when you do not have the time is not the way forward, no matter how badly you want it. There are no easy, magic fixes to create more time or prevent the problems that will be caused by leaving a puppy unsupervised for prolonged periods. We really wish there were!

Puppy's First Night
By Sally Bradbury

It doesn't matter where puppy sleeps at night as long as it's with you. Your new puppy has left his mum and siblings and everything he has ever known in his short life so far. He's never been alone before, and you need to provide comfort and security until puppy is confident enough to be alone if this is your goal.

Well-meaning friends and family (and maybe even the breeder) will tell you to put puppy in the crate and leave him alone to cry. There is simply no need to cause a puppy to get upset in order to teach him to be OK alone. It will have the opposite effect to the one you are looking for. Leaving a puppy to 'cry it out' will result in an anxious, less healthy, fearful dog. Studies have shown that infants of any social species who have their needs met are far more likely to become confident and independent and that 'crying it out' can lead to dependence and, ultimately, an adult dog with full blown separation anxiety. Be prepared for this to take several weeks or even months with some puppies. Do not rush it as a puppy will have several false starts in confidence.

For the best possible night's sleep all round, take puppy to bed with you once he has eaten supper, been out to the toilet, and is ready to fall asleep. For those first few nights, sleep while puppy sleeps.

You may choose to cuddle puppy to sleep and then place him in a crate once asleep. This can be on the bed (against the wall), or next to the bed, either raised to your bed height or on the floor beside you. You will then be able to reach the crate to dangle a reassuring finger in it.

You may find it preferable to cuddle puppy on the bed if he needs the close contact. He'll be safe between two people or against the wall with one person.

You will wake up if he wakes needing the toilet, but the more contented and soundly puppy sleeps, the less likely he is to wake.

If you do not want puppy in the bedroom because you co-sleep with children, or perhaps it is the cat's territory, then one of you can sleep on the sofa with puppy, or with puppy in a crate or pen next to the sofa.

You will be right there for him when he wakes to take him out to the toilet and to cuddle him back to sleep again if it's still dark outside. If the sun is up then you may decide, along with the puppy, that the day needs to start!

Cry It Out?
Why what we learnt from children applies to puppies
By Emma Judson

Since at least 1913, there has been a school of thought that suggests leaving tiny babies to 'cry it out', that is, cry until they give up crying, with the parent no longer responding to cries for attention, comfort or contact, is beneficial or indeed, necessary in raising children.

At some point, this also became the advice applied to puppies, with warnings that if you respond to a pup's cries for attention, you would, as with the child-oriented version of this advice, create a needy individual who was insecure and lacking in confidence.

We now know the opposite is true. Unfortunately (from the perspective of canine behaviour), very few studies are done on dogs crying it out. This is simply because there isn't money in carrying them out.

So, we are left to extrapolate from studies done on children. That's actually OK, because a dog's brain is comparable to the brain of a child under two years of age. They have similar needs for comfort, warmth, food, physical contact, and social support. They have similar difficulties in communicating orally, and they both lack impulse control and fine motor skills.

So, here's the grim truth.

Young mammals left to 'cry it out' do not 'self soothe'. In fact, what they learn is that after going through a cycle of protestation, then despair, they reach a third phase of detachment (Bowlby J. 1960s). In effect, they give up trying to get a response, get comfort or contact and become apathetic. Their distress is still present; they have simply learnt it will not be alleviated as a result of their behaviour. They have shut down.

The theory ran that if you provided attention constantly or responded promptly to their cries, so that the young mammal in question did not need to cry, they would cry even more and seek more attention. In fact, the opposite is true.

A study in 1986 showed that the more the mother holds and carries her baby, the less that baby will cry and fuss. Other studies (cross-cultural but still human, not dog) showed that those parents who responded quicker to crying babies also had babies who cried far less often!

Going back to puppies, we have taken them from their mothers, their littermates, and their familiar environment.

If we compare our domestic dog to feral and wild dog populations, we see that our domestic puppies generally experience this separation from their primary caregiver and littermates at between six and 12 weeks of age.

Their wild/feral counterparts are in the constant company of littermates and the near constant company of their parents until weaning. Beyond weaning, they are still in the constant company of littermates, parents, and other relatives unless they choose to be alone. This is unlikely to happen before adolescence and the related hormonal changes.

It is true that domestic dogs and wild or feral canids are not the same, but the difference is that domestic dogs actively want to be with humans rather than with other canids. That being so, they are in no way equipped to be isolated and alone, any more than the feral or wild dogs would be.

So, what are the risks of subjecting a puppy to isolation from a social group or new primary caregiver and ignoring cries for company, comfort, or contact?

- The increased cortisol levels can actually damage or kill off neurons and the neuronal interconnections. This can affect how well your dog copes with stress, anxiety, and fear in the future, predisposing them to be more reactive and fearful
- Stress hormones go up faster than they come back down. So, that stressful experience is affecting the dog for much longer than you might think. Possibly days
- Repeatedly increasing stress hormones will inhibit learning, affect sleep, affect bonding and attachment
- Repeated stressful experiences that the subject cannot escape from lead to PTSD in humans. We have no evidence to suggest that this does not also happen in dogs. Given the similarities between the human and canine brain, it is reasonable to assume dogs can also experience something similar to PTSD

The short version of all this is: there is no benefit to leaving a dog to 'cry it out'. Separation anxiety is normal for puppies; they need to be with someone most of the time!

Separation anxiety is an abnormal behavioural issue that comes about because of an insecure dog, who has not been taught how to cope by themselves, not as a result of creating a secure, confident dog who is given what they need as a puppy.

Raising a Puppy

The force-free way to a happy, confident pup, and a great relationship

By Sally Bradbury

There are four steps to a harmonious relationship:

1. Prevent
2. Reinforce
3. Teach
4. Interrupt Positively

Prevent

Prevent what you can wherever possible and manage the pup's environment so that he has little or no opportunity to go wrong. This means puppy-proofing the house and includes moving books from the lower shelves on the bookshelves (I had to relocate the bottles in the wine rack in the kitchen when my pup was younger!!), putting bins behind cupboard doors, picking up all Persian rugs temporarily, using stair gates, and closing doors to prevent access to areas where the pup may chew precious furnishings. Most importantly, it involves putting things away, such as shoes and children's toys.

Any time your dog engages in an unwanted behaviour, take a step back and ask yourself how you could have prevented it.

Reinforce

Reinforce your pup for offering behaviours that are agreeable. This can even be the absence of an unwanted behaviour. The best way to do this is to have a pot of small, yummy treats, such as hot dog sausage, liver, or cheese, say 30 in number, and set yourself a challenge to catch your dog doing something that you like, and would like him to do again, 30 times during the day. It could be lying in his bed, choosing to keep his front feet on the floor when a visitor comes in, coming in from the garden, chewing his chew toy; the possibilities are endless (think I nicked that from an advert). To start with, you may struggle to find 30 opportunities. However, as dogs do what works for them, you will soon need more treats in that pot because your dog is going to be throwing these behaviours at you left, right and centre. These are behaviours that you haven't asked for, by the way, and this is by far the easiest way for a dog to learn.

Teach

Teach your dog what you would like him to do. The obvious things are to walk nicely on a lead, come when called, sit, lie down, and stay. There are lots of ways to teach your dog, but it is important that whatever method you choose, it is easy to understand and fair to the dog. Think back to how you learned in school. I bet your favourite subject was the one where the teacher made it fun and enjoyable to learn and motivated you with praise and rewards for good work. I tend to teach all of my dogs during play, so lots of fetch and tug games used as rewards and the dog is having a ton of fun while learning.

Interrupt Unwanted Behaviour

I know from experience that it is not always possible to prevent all unwanted behaviours when you have a puppy.

It is very difficult not to get cross when your pup chews your smartphone or expensive shoes; it is human nature. However, in terms of your relationship with your dog and ensuring that the behaviour doesn't continue into adulthood, you really do have to take a deep breath and try not to scowl. The damage is done, and nothing will undo it now.

So, you teach your dog a positive interrupter. This can be a word or a noise, anything you like, as long as it doesn't frighten or startle your pup. My pup's positive interrupter is 'Moss' said in a happy voice. I can use his name because I have never said it crossly or to tell him off. You could use a 'Yay!!' or a kissy noise for example. All you do is use food treats, you can move to a toy later, and say the word as you give him a treat. Repeat a few hundred times. Yes, really! Now watch his response to that word next time you say it when he is doing something you would like to interrupt. Once interrupted redirect him onto something more productive.

If you interrupt unwanted behaviours in a way that frightens your dog, he will simply learn that these behaviours are dangerous to do when you are present and will seek opportunities to engage in them when your back is turned. And yes, the dog could learn to engage in the behaviours in order to be positively interrupted, BUT he will only do it when you are watching. No point when you are not, so now you can interrupt before the damage is done. Meanwhile, teach the dog a more rewarding behaviour instead.

Think of your relationship with your puppy as a bank account. Every positive interaction is a deposit; every time you punish you make a withdrawal. As soon as your account becomes overdrawn, then things will just go from bad to worse. Keep a nice healthy bank balance and you and you pup will soon end up as millionaires in the relationship stakes.

Toilet Training
By Sally Bradbury

Toilet training is all about creating good habits. Young pups have very small bladders and very little bladder control, so they need to be in the right place when nature calls. To toilet train successfully in as short a time as possible, you must take your puppy to the garden:

- When they wake
- After eating
- After taking a drink
- Before, during and after a period of activity
- When you come in
- Before you go out
- Before bedtime
- During the adverts
- And every twenty to thirty minutes in between unless they are asleep. During periods of activity, change that to every ten to twenty minutes

Stay outdoors with your pup. Do not nag or distract him. Just mooch about and he will do the same and eventually eliminate. Quiet praise is sufficient.

Once pup has eliminated, you can either stay out and play or go back indoors. If you stay out for a game, then he will often need to go again before you go back indoors. So, stop the game and stay out for a while longer to give him a chance to go again. If puppy doesn't eliminate outdoors after a few minutes, take him back in and sit him on your lap or, if he is a small breed, tuck him under your arm as you go about your chores. Try again in five minutes. It is imperative that you do this, especially if you have started off by laying down newspaper or puppy pads because your puppy may prefer to pee indoors, and he could simply be waiting to be taken back in.

Give him zero opportunity to go wrong. If your puppy toilets in the house, it is because you haven't toilet trained him yet and didn't take him outdoors when he needed to go. When this happens take a rolled-up newspaper and hit yourself over the head while repeating the words 'I forgot to watch my puppy. I forgot to watch my puppy'. If your puppy laughs at you when you do this – praise him.

Common Mistakes During Toilet Training

- *Using newspaper or puppy training pads*
  While it may aid the cleaning up process it can be very confusing for a pup that is taught or allowed to toilet in the house to then make the transition to going outdoors. It will often result in a pup that, when playing in the garden, will simply hold on until they are back indoors, because that is where the toilet is
- *Leaving the door open*
  Without a physical barrier, there is no difference between outdoors and indoors
- *Reprimands for toileting in the house*
  This will result in a dog that believes you disapprove of what he did, not **where** he did it, and is damaging to your relationship with your pup
- *Giving treats for toileting in the garden*
  Again the dog is being rewarded for what he did, not where he did it. While this is not going to be as big a problem as the reprimand, the clever dog will learn to do lots of little wees and never fully empty their bladder. The insecure dog may wee indoors to appease you if you get cross about something else because they know that this is something that pleases you and gets rewarded. NOTE: using both reprimands and rewards for eliminating is very confusing for your pup
- *Expecting your pup to tell you when he needs to go out*
  Once a pup understands that outdoors is where the toilet is, then he may start to let you know he needs to go out. However, if you are not there to ask or you fail to notice him asking, then the house training will break down. It's far better to have a dog go out to the toilet on your schedule once they are toilet trained
- *Giving your pup an en-suite in his crate*
  Do not encourage your pup to toilet in his crate by putting puppy pads in there. If you have to leave puppy for a while and he is going to need to go, then it's best to have the crate inside a larger pen or blocked off area and leave the crate door open so that he can get away from his bed to toilet.

Areas indoors where pup has had an accident are best cleaned with a dilute solution of biological washing powder/laundry detergent, which contains enzymes. Avoid using disinfectant that contains ammonia as this will encourage pup to pee there again.

No puppy is going to be reliably toilet trained under about seven to eight months old. That doesn't mean that you will have regular accidents in the house, just that they are still learning and if there are accidents, it is human error.

Overnight

Young pups will need to go to the toilet once or twice in the night for anything from a few days to a few weeks.

If your pup is sleeping in a crate in the bedroom with you, then they will wake and should let you know they need to go out. Carry pup to the garden to eliminate and then straight back to bed again. A few nights of this, and it will take you longer to find your slippers because of sleep deprivation. Consequently, pup is learning to hold on and will soon be sleeping all night. If you choose to leave puppy in the kitchen or utility room to sleep, then do not shut them in a crate and simply clean up in the morning without comment.

Why Punishment Doesn't Work for Toilet Training

A typical morning in the life of an eight-week-old pup:

- 7:00 am: Puppy pees in the garden – Owner present. Gets praised
- 7:30 am: Puppy pees in the kitchen – Owner present. Gets a reprimand
- 8:15 am: Puppy pees in the lounge – Owner not present. Nothing happens except relief
- 9:00 am: Puppy pees in the lounge – Owner present. Gets a reprimand
- 9:30 am: Puppy pees in the kitchen – Owner not present. Nothing, just relief
- 11:00 am: Puppy pees in the garden – Owner doesn't notice. Just relief again
- 11:30 am: Puppy pees under the dining room table – Owner not present. Nothing happens
- 12:15 pm: Puppy pees in the garden – Owner present. Gets praise

What we think we are teaching puppy is that it is good to pee in the garden and wrong to pee in the house. What the pup is actually learning, is that sometimes it is rewarding to pee when the owner is present and sometimes it is dangerous. However, it is always safe to go when the owner is not present and, so far, the safest place is under the dining room table.

Never deny your dog water in the mistaken belief that this will aid toilet training. It won't. It will make the urine stronger and may affect your dog's health. It could cause kidney problems or urinary tract infections if the dog drinks greedily and excessively when it is available, knowing it will be taken away. Dogs must have clean fresh water available all the time.

Puppy Biting

By Kate Harland

OK people, I'm going to tell you the truth. The awful, irrefutable truth that every prospective puppy owner should be made to write out 5,000 times until it haunts their dreams. The truth is: PUPPIES BITE! I know we'd prefer them not to, but expecting your puppy not to bite is a bit like expecting your six-month-old baby not to dribble. It's just not going to happen.

Puppies bite simply because it's how they learn about the world. Just as babies put everything in their mouths, puppies bite everything in sight. It's also a really important method of communication for them. Most puppy nipping is their way of encouraging you to play with them, exactly the same as a toddler pulling at your sleeve and saying, 'Mummy, play with me please!' It may not be convenient, but that doesn't stop them asking!

Puppy biting isn't usually anything to do with teething. Puppies rarely have discomfort or pain with teething, and the first thing most puppy owners know about it is when they find a recently lost puppy tooth on the carpet! Don't believe me? Have a look at how many of the 'articles' online about puppy teething discomfort are actually trying to sell you something like teething gel, or the latest super-duper teething chew toy. It's clever marketing, but no more than that. If you want to give your pup frozen dishrags or carrots to chew on, then fine. If they like them, then it's another texture to add to their experience, but it won't necessarily confirm that they had any discomfort.

Puppies will also growl and sometimes bite if they're afraid or threatened, much as any other animal will. A pup who's scared will often back away and growl; the adrenaline is preparing his body for 'fight or flight'. If the threat continues and he can't escape, he'll bite. Just one more reason not to use 'correction', stern voices, or aversive training methods with your pup.

So, let's look at the constant 'play with me!' biting that we're all so familiar with. What can we do? Well, your pup has no idea that it's not OK to drag at your clothes, nip your hands, or try to catch your bare ankles. It's just fun! And the more you squeal, move your feet, and try to detach his teeth from your best shirt, the more fun it is. It's your job to teach him that more appropriate play is just as much fun.

First, let's look at what doesn't work. Pointing a wagging finger at your pup and telling them off in a stern voice is worse than useless. Not only because your pup has no idea why you're doing it, but the stern voice and aggressive body language will simply make him anxious and frustrated, which in turn exacerbates the situation. Saying 'no bite' might help you to feel as if you're doing something about it, but 'it's all pineapples to dogs' so don't waste your breath. Putting them in time out doesn't teach them anything. Don't waste a teaching opportunity. If it's a choice between time out behind a baby gate or throttling the pup because you're so frustrated, then go for time out. Don't think it will help your pup to understand that you don't want him to bite though, because it won't. And don't punish your pup by shutting him in his crate (if he has one), as that will undo all the work that you're hopefully doing, teaching him that his crate is a wonderful, happy, cosy place to be, and not a prison.

Rip up an old sheet or towel into strips, plait the strips or tie big chewy knots spaced out along the length, and teach him to play tuggy. Teach him cue words such as 'get it' or 'drop', whatever you choose, to indicate the start and end of the game. That way, you can teach him that it's a reciprocal game, you wiggle it, he gets it. You ask him to drop it, he does. The game starts again. All good for learning lots of other activities. Make the tuggy long enough to keep your hands away from his teeth. Some pups prefer you to hold both ends and they catch the middle. Keep the focus on the floor, not dangling in the air. If a fabric tuggy doesn't float his boat, try tying his favourite toy onto a long cord, or experiment with a flirt pole.

For ankle biters, wellies will become your best friend! Clean wellies to wear in the house will discourage him from biting and will protect your ankles so the yelping and jumping stops. No fun for pup! And like the majority of unwanted behaviours, if you can prevent pup practising it, he'll forget about it in time.

Now, I know we all have busy lives, but the more you can play with your puppy, the less he'll have to 'encourage' you to play at times that really aren't convenient. Young puppies can sleep for up to 19 hours out of the 24, so when he is awake try to focus on him. It's an investment that will pay dividends in the future.

'But what about the children?' I hear you ask. 'Why does my pup insist on chasing the children and pulling at their clothes, until they're scared of him? This isn't what I expected!' Well, let's look at it from your pup's point of view. There's you, with a soft, gentle voice, and you feed him, and stroke him, and calm him down. Then there are smaller creatures with high pitched voices like squeaky toys, and they move quickly and yelp and jump up and down and they're just soooo exciting!

Unfortunately, the wonderful images you see on TV of little children and puppies playing beautifully together are usually staged and, in most cases, this really doesn't happen. Your children and your pup will have loads of time to be best friends later on when he's grown up a bit, but just as you'd never leave human toddlers playing together unsupervised, you really need to oversee all the interaction between your pup and your children.

The good news, of course, is that it eventually stops. Some pups stop biting fairly quickly if other games are more fun. Some decide that it's staying part of their repertoire as long as you're happy with it. My youngest dog is eighteen months old now but still mouths our hands and we don't have a problem with that.

Puppy Biting and Play
By Sally Bradbury

Biting is a normal puppy behaviour. Puppies investigate the world through their mouths. If it's within reach, it will probably be picked up and chewed! If it is exciting and moves fast, it will definitely get bitten. Dogs play by using their mouths because they don't have hands.

Puppies need to bite, and they need to play. What he is doing is simply trying to elicit play. Play is by far the best way to bond with your pup and is a great way to reward him while learning, so you don't really want to tell your puppy you don't want to play with him.

Don't get cross. Don't make noises that may startle or excite him more. Don't ignore him or use time-outs, as this is time wasted that could be used to teach him how to play appropriately. Don't just give him a toy to play with. If he's biting you, it's because he wants to play with you, not with a toy on his own.

Use tug toys that he can bite; old, knotted towels, or a favourite toy with string attached. Unwanted dressing gown cords are ideal. You need to encourage him to bite one end of the toy, while you hold the other end. You can then have a great game together without getting bitten.

Ensure your tug toys are long enough and soft enough for your puppy to happily bite. Your toy should touch the floor while you are holding the other end. This allows you to animate the toy and keep the game low to the ground, so as not to encourage your pup to jump up. It also puts distance between teeth and hands.

Keep these interactive toys out of your pup's reach while they are not being played with. It will keep them more novel, which means the pup is more likely to want to bite and play with them when given the opportunity. Plant toys around the house and garden (out of puppy's reach), so you have them easily accessible. As much as possible, take the game outdoors.

Rotate chew items that you leave on the floor to also keep them interesting.

Do not play with your puppy unless you have a toy for him to grab. Don't let anyone roughhouse with him or roll about on the floor with him.

Invest in a puppy pen for young pups so that they can be safely confined for short periods, especially if you have children. This also provides a barrier that you can play through with a long tug toy before puppy has learned to bite toys, not body parts.

Start by animating the toy on the floor and saying 'get it' every time your pup grabs the toy. You hold on to the toy and let him grab it and shake it. Let go of the toy sometimes so that puppy is encouraged to come back to you to start the game again.

At some point, you can also teach a word for letting go. To do this, you simply stop the game by putting a finger in pup's collar and keep hold of the toy. Release the pressure on the toy so that it becomes boring. As soon as pup lets go, say 'thank you' and immediately invite him to grab it again with a 'get it'. He will quickly learn to let go when you stop playing for the game to start again. Eventually the word 'thank you' (or your word of choice) will become his cue to let go.

Once your pup is getting the idea of the game, then you can start to add in a 'sit' and an 'are you ready' before the 'get it'. Before you know it, you have a dog sitting and waiting patiently for the game to start.

Games to Play with Your Puppy
By Sally Bradbury

Tug

Play gentle games of tug with your puppy. Use a long soft toy; rope or fleece is ideal. Animate the toy on the floor and encourage puppy to grab it. You just need to hold it and be part of the fun. There is no need to pull or shake the toy; let puppy do that.

Playing tug has many advantages, not least in giving him an outlet for his play biting. By putting it on cue you can teach a puppy what to bite and when to bite, which is much better than trying to insist on no biting at all during play. After all that's how puppies play. They have no hands.

Fetch

Gently roll a soft ball or toy across the ground and encourage puppy to chase, pick it up, and bring it back.

There are a hundred and one uses for a dog that retrieves. Perhaps the biggest advantage is that you can completely avoid triggering the guarding behaviour that is often associated with having to take an item from him that he has picked up but shouldn't have. Using praise and encouragement, just as you would with his toy, will see him willingly bringing the forbidden item to you.

Find It

Let puppy watch you hide a toy and then encourage him to find it. Progress onto hiding it unseen and let puppy do what comes naturally and use his nose to search. Every family needs a dog that can find misplaced keys.

Socialising: The Good, The Bad and The Consequences
Or raising a happy, confident, well-rounded puppy
By Sally Bradbury

Everyone knows the importance of socialising a puppy, but it isn't always easy to get it right. Check below to see if you are on the right track:

Choosing Your Puppy
Good
- Research your chosen breed
- Choose a reputable breeder or rescue
- Be prepared for the third degree from the breeder or rescue
- Be prepared to go on a waiting list for a puppy
- See the litter with Mum at least once before buying, and details (including a picture) of Dad

Bad
- Buying a puppy from an online advert
- Buying a puppy from an 'all singing, all dancing' website that always has puppies available
- Buying a puppy from someone who will sell to you without checking your suitability
- Buying an older puppy that the breeder has hung onto before deciding that they are not going to keep it, but did not socialise
- Deciding you want a puppy and buying one tomorrow

Consequences
A happy, confident, well-rounded puppy…

… or run the risk that your puppy has been raised in squalid conditions with a sickly, nervous, stressed Mum; stress that has affected the puppies in-utero and in the nest.

People
Good
- Take puppy out in your arms or a sling and watch people from a safe distance. Do this in many different environments, all within your puppy's comfort zone
- Always allow puppy the choice to interact with people or not

Bad
- 'Pass the puppy' at puppy class
- Letting strangers approach and touch your puppy
- Encouraging people to pick up your puppy
- Allowing people to 'discipline' your puppy

Consequences
A happy, confident, well-rounded puppy…

... or a puppy that is scared or wary of strangers, and is reactive to people out on walks or visitors in the home...

... or a puppy that runs up to people in the park, jumps all over visitors, has zero manners and zero recall.

Dogs
Good
- Walks and play dates with carefully selected, sensible adult dogs and other compatible pups
- A good puppy class with the emphasis on dog/owner interaction in the company of others

Bad
- Puppy parties
- Puppy classes with free-for-all play sessions
- Dog parks
- Encouraging or allowing your on-lead puppy to approach unknown dogs
- Letting your puppy play with every dog they meet at the park
- Getting two puppies at the same time or a few months apart and letting them entertain each other all day
- Allowing a puppy to spend all day with, and be a pest to, an older dog
- Letting other dogs 'teach him a lesson'

Consequences
A happy, confident, well-rounded puppy...

... or a puppy that is scared or wary of dogs and becomes reactive to dogs when out...

... or a puppy that thinks every dog he sees is his best mate, runs to dogs when off lead and is reactive when on lead, has zero manners, and zero recall.

The importance of early socialising cannot be overemphasised. This must be done carefully and considerately, while ensuring that stress is kept to a minimum. Experiences should be positive, as well as being in the best interests of the puppy. This will ensure that he/she grows up to be a happy, confident, well-rounded dog.

Socialising and Social Distancing

Written during the 2020/21 Covid-19 pandemic

By Sally Bradbury

If you have a new puppy, there is no need to worry unduly about how you are going to socialise him/her in the current situation.

Socialising is not just about playing with other dogs or meeting lots of people. Being sociable is about being able to walk politely past people and dogs. Now, with social distancing, we have the perfect opportunity to take puppy out without having to worry about puppy being frightened by a boisterous 'he only wants to play' dog. Nor by being overwhelmed by the attention he attracts from strangers and exuberant children. Or conversely, teaching him that every dog he sees is a playmate, and every person a new best friend.

Whether your puppy is a shy introvert or a confident extrovert, you can take puppy out in your arms, a sling, or in the car and find somewhere to sit and watch the world go by. Pup can eat treats and play with you.

Puppy can get used to traffic, seeing people, dogs, and farm animals, all from a safe distance. This can continue as he gets older and is walking on harness and lead or can go off lead or on a line for a run about. Try and visit as many different locations as you can during the first few weeks.

Socialising is about your puppy experiencing a variety of different settings, situations, and encounters. They do not need to be in the thick of it to do so, and often feel more comfortable watching from the side-lines. We might even find that the current generation of puppies grow up to be more well-rounded, as they were allowed to experience new things at a safe distance, and perhaps had fewer scary encounters.

NB: This was written at the beginning of the coronavirus pandemic.

Crate Training

Step-by-step guide to a distress free, force-free, crate trained dog or pup

By Emma Judson

Please sit and read this guide thoroughly before making a start, as it is important that every single step of this is carried out and nothing is skipped.

It is also important to understand, before you start, *why* it is vital to crate train your dog.

Crates are often seen as a place to lock a naughty dog, or a place where dogs are left shut away for long hours. It is true that they can be misused just like any other item of dog-related equipment.

However, once properly trained, your dog can find being crated reassuring, and a visual cue to relax and go to sleep.

Crates can be used to aid in toilet training, dealing with fear or reactivity, introducing new dogs, and in rehabilitation from illness or injury. Crates are commonly used when transporting dogs, at the groomers, and, of course, in a veterinary surgery or hospital.

Unless you can guarantee that your dog is never going to travel, be groomed, go to the vet's, or require strict and confined rest – something you can only do if you can see the future – then your dog needs to know how to handle being crated!

Crate training will never involve your dog being shut in against his will. There will be no crying or whining or scrabbling or barking in an attempt to get out of the crate. If there are any of the above signs, you are not following the instructions correctly.

You will need: One wire crate, appropriately sized for your dog, with a bed or blanket inside. If you have a large breed puppy who is currently tiny, a small crate (which is big enough for your dog right now) is OK for training purposes. One pot of very high-value treats. Try cheese, hot dog, or chicken – whatever your dog likes best. One food dispensing toy, such as a Kong.

Step 1: Crate = Treats

- Sit beside the open doorway of the crate
- The door should be wide open – as far as it will go
- Ideally, you should sit at the side of the crate where the door would latch shut
- Have your pot of treats with you and, of course, your dog or puppy
- Show your dog the treats if necessary, and then toss one treat into the crate
- Your dog should follow the treat into the crate to eat it
- A dog or pup who has never seen a crate before, or who has and is generally OK with the idea, will go straight in
- A dog or pup who has already been terrified of a crate, or is generally nervous, may not go straight in. If this is the case, put the treat right by the door and start with rewarding them for just approaching the crate
- It is really important to note that your dog or pup *can* come straight out of the crate once they have eaten the treat. It is entirely *their* choice
- The rule is super simple. Going into the crate earns a treat. Not going into the crate, or coming out of the crate, doesn't earn a treat
- Even the daftest of dogs can work out the very simple maths here. In crate = goodies. Out of crate = 0 goodies
- Play the 'treats are in the crate' game for a few minutes. If you only get a pup zooming in and out of the crate happily for treats, that is fine at this stage
- If you get a pup or adult dog who goes into the crate, then hovers to see if more treats will happen without them having to come out and go in again, reward that! Put more treats in *before* your dog comes out again
- Ideally, we want the dog to hang around inside the crate, hoping for more treats. If he does that, he has chosen to be in there of his own free will! So, reward that
- Keep tossing in treats and praising your dog, but don't be tempted to shut that door yet!

Step 2: Crate = More Treats

By the end of the first session or two, your dog is hopefully starting to think that hanging around in the crate might be an easy way to earn more treats.

If he isn't, continue with step one.

For step two, sit slightly to the side of the crate and, when he goes in for his first treat, start popping a treat or two through the bars. This is why we are using a wire crate and not a fabric one!

Your dog is probably still going in the crate and remaining standing, so now I would put two or three treats further back into the crate and see if he lies down to eat them. If he *does*, reward that with a small handful through the bars, ideally delivered so that he doesn't have to get up to reach them. Give lots of praise for this.

When he is going in and lying down and clearly expecting treats to be delivered, you can begin to pause for just a fraction of a second before doing so. This is the how you begin to build up the time he stays in the crate.

Again, remember to keep *away* from that crate door; forget it even exists for the time being.

Step 3: Moving Around – You, Not Him

By now, your dog should be zooming into the crate and lying down. He probably won't need to be bribed in there with a treat, but he will still need treats for going in and staying in there.

Vary the length of time he waits for his treat. So, lots of times he gets the treats almost straight away, and sometimes he waits for a few seconds or even up to one minute.

When you are at that level, you can begin to shift your position while he is inside the crate. This means you can shuffle further away or to the side to begin with, then shuffle back and reward him for having done nothing. The reality is, of course, that he has done a wonderful thing; he's chosen to stay in the crate despite you moving.

Remember to move only a tiny bit and move in whichever direction or fashion is *least* likely to encourage him to move – hence shuffling rather than standing up at this stage. It's also important to remember to keep the time you spend 'away' very brief, so you may even need to just lean your body away, then back, and then reward before shuffling away. Then you can slowly work on edging away.

Step 4: Find your Feet

You are ready for this stage if you can lean, shuffle, or edge away from your dog in the crate, in a variety of directions. This should be for a minimum of 30 seconds, and ideally a maximum of around two minutes, before you return and reward him.

Watch your dog carefully now. Does he look relaxed and comfortable? Or does he look like he's ready to spring up and out of the crate? You want relaxed and comfortable. If he is looking anxious and ready to spring up and out, go back a bit. Reduce the frequency, the distance, or the time you are away. Possibly all three. Increase the value of the reward, too, so that it's more fun for him.

It is really important not to skip this stage or rush it, because now you are going to be standing up instead of sitting by the crate. Initially, you want to start out sitting and stand up while he is in there.

Wait until he is relaxed in the crate. Stand up slowly and drop in a few treats by bending over. Then squat or kneel back down. You can sit if it's easy for you to jump up and down from sitting.

For this stage, you are *just* going to be working on kneeling/squatting near the cage, and then standing up and rewarding, and back down again. Do not step away from the crate at this point.

Mix it up with work from the earlier steps. So, sometimes sit and reward for him staying, sometimes sit and lean away, or sit and bum-shuffle away and back, and reward.

It is important that going in the crate does not become an accurate predictor or visual cue that tells your dog you will be leaving, because if your dog has an issue with being left, this will be a big problem. Mix up the work, so that sometimes the reward is for something your dog finds easy to cope with, and sometimes it's for something he finds harder. Resist the trap of making his task harder and harder every single time because that leads to dogs predicting and becoming sour to the lesson you are teaching.

Step 5: Stepping Away

Now you should have a dog who really couldn't give a damn if you are sat there, sat a foot away, bum-shuffling around, leaning in and out, standing up, or squatting down. All he knows is, he's in the crate and he gets treats for stopping in there, and that's good!

If your crate is located where it is available for your dog to go into at any time, you should find that he will choose to go in there, even outside of a training session. If that is the case, randomly reward him for that. Just walk by and drop a tasty morsel in to him. You could also offer him his meals or treat-filled Kongs in there now.

The next step is to ask him to go in the crate and then you stand up and step away. Just one step, and then step back and reward. Build that up over the course of several sessions until you can take several steps away, pause, return, and reward, and he doesn't bat an eyelid.

Really resist the urge to shut him in there now. There's a good chance you'd get away with it at this stage, but you could easily cause a problem if he panics. The last thing we want is him learning that he *can't* get out. That would make him fear the crate.

Step 6: Going Away

You should not be starting this step until your dog or pup is belting into the crate, lying down, falling asleep in there, happy to eat meals or treats in there, offering you 'I'm in my crate' behaviours and is actually sometimes found in the crate when you have been out of the room.

So, for this session, start with your dog in the crate. Reward him, step away, step back, reward him, walk around the crate, reward him, and step outside the door (ideally an internal door) or otherwise pop out of sight for just a split second, then back without much in the way of fuss, and reward him.

Repeat this and mix it up again, as we did before, so that going in the crate does not necessarily mean you will be leaving the room or going out of sight.

Keep working on this stage until you can leave the room for a few minutes. You could leave and go to another floor of your house. Or you could leave the room *and* leave the house. All for just a few minutes. On your return, your dog should still be in the crate.

You may need to set up your crate in another room or use a phone or webcam to record him.

If possible, practise some of the earlier stages in other rooms of your home. This isn't always possible because not every home has several rooms with space for a crate and for you to work around it. If you *can*, it will really help your dog generalise that the crate is cool, no matter where it is. When changing location, the golden rule is to step back down a level or two, so that the work is a little easier. This is to compensate for the new location, which makes things a little harder.

At this point, if you come back and your dog is **not** in the crate, I would say nothing. If you can't resist, I'd go to the empty crate and act as if I'm going to put a treat in there, but then act silly – *'Oh there is no dog here. Oh dear!'*, and pocket the treat. This *very* much depends on your dog. Some of my dogs would be *'OMG I should have been in there… doh!',* and some wouldn't give a rat's. But there are dogs who might be upset by this behaviour. If that's the case, don't do this.

Whatever sort of dog you have though, if you come in and the dog is not in the crate, then it's likely you have gone too fast. You've probably tried to be out too long, or too far away. The *important* thing here is to make a note of that, go back a step or two, and spend a bit more time working on an earlier level. It is not the end of the world if this happens. No one died, so don't get upset and certainly, do not get angry.

Step 7: Closing the Door

OMG, yes really!

So, now you should have a dog who loves his crate, wants to be in his crate, and stays in his crate, hoping for his reward, while you move around the home.

Now you will go *allllll* the way back down to step one, but you will push the crate door closed gently. You will be sat by the crate again as you were at the beginning, putting treats through the bars of the crate.

Here's the really important part: the split second your dog approaches the door, reaches out to nudge it or paw it or push it – you fling that door open *fast. You* do that. You do *not* at any stage, ever, wait for your dog to try to get the door open themselves.

So, let's say your dog approached the crate door and you flung it wide open for him. He has probably come out and looked at you like, *'what?'*

Say nothing, just give your dog a second or two and see if *he* offers 'going in the crate'. If he does, reward him. If he doesn't within a second or two, then toss a treat in the crate and start again.

What your dog is learning here is that he is *never, ever* trapped in the crate, even if it looks like he is. You are opening the door and releasing him before he *feels* trapped, but there is no reward for coming out.

In the long-term, your dog won't care if the door is open or closed, because being in the crate has always been rewarding. Coming out has never been an issue and isn't rewarding.

If a dog *is* ever trapped in a crate, two things happen. Firstly, they feel fear and they distrust the crate. Secondly, when they get out, coming *out* has then been extremely rewarding. The relief from feeling trapped in there is massively reinforcing.

By never allowing your dog to feel trapped, you also never allow him to feel that relief.

Gradually re-work your way through all the steps with the door pushed closed, but really importantly at this point, *not latched shut*.

You will need to stay near enough to the crate that you can flip the door open fast. Work steadily enough that you are sure your dog won't try to get out before you are ready to release him.

Step 8: Locking the Door

So, to recap, by now you should have a dog who will stay in the crate with the door open or the door pushed closed, whether you are in the room or you have popped in and out or stepped out for a few minutes.

He should be really relaxed in there and want to remain in there for the rewards you will still be giving him. He should also be used to some period of waiting before those rewards happen.

He should never have tried to get out of the crate by pushing, nudging, or pawing at the door.

If your dog *has* done that, don't panic. Go back a few stages and re-do the foundations again and go a little slower. If you are keeping a diary of your progress, you may be able to pinpoint where you rushed something or where something went a bit wrong.

So, to introduce the door being locked, go back a few steps, probably to stepping away and stepping in and out of the room. This time, after a few goes with the door pushed shut, lock it, wait a few seconds without moving, then unlock it, and continue the session.

I would *not* end a session immediately after opening the crate door. Instead, throughout the session, mix up closing and locking the door with leaving the door open. This means he is not predicting the door being unlocked and opened as either a release cue, or cue for his reward and end of session.

Step 9: Increasing the Time he can be Crated

By now, you should have a dog who is totally happy to go in his crate, have the door pushed shut, randomly earn rewards in there, have the door locked while you move around the room, step outside the room and even the house, for up to around four or five minutes.

Now you build duration for real, sometimes leaving him for slightly longer. Again, try not to do this as a neat linear progression. Do not leave him for five minutes on day one and 10 minutes on day two and 15 minutes on day three, as the chances are he's going to predict that the crate now means being left and that's not fun for him.

Instead, mix things up. Maybe he's in there for five minutes on day one, but on day two you just potter around in the same room as the crate. Maybe on day three he's in there for 10 minutes, but you are in and out of the house (unloading shopping perhaps), on day four you only do five minutes, but you are sitting reading a magazine and mostly ignoring him.

The point is, it's gradual, but it's no big deal for him. It's not a predictor for something awful.

Because he has never felt trapped, because he's never felt any reinforcing relief at being released from the crate, being in the crate is not a big deal. The fact that he *can't* come out at this point is totally irrelevant to him because he does not *want* to come out in the first place.

Beyond Step Nine

If you have a crate and will use it regularly, it's a good idea to keep rewarding your dog for being in there, even after he seems totally comfy about it. It's also a good idea to pop him in there for a minute or two when you answer the door, or when a guest comes in, or to give him a tasty bone – just so that he feels it's a wonderful place to be, and it doesn't mean you are going out.

If you don't have a crate set up all the time, do get your crate out from time to time and practise with it. That way, it is not a shock to him when a non-doggy visitor comes to stay and you need to use it, or when he has to go to the vets, or you are going to take him on holiday and need to use it there.

Never use your crate as a place to shut a dog as punishment. It must stay a safe and rewarding place and he must *like* being in there. It should go without saying that you should not abuse your dog's good nature and shut him in there for more than four hours at a time. It will take you some time, probably months with a puppy, to work up to that length of time anyway.

Do not allow anyone to tease or torment your dog when he is in the crate. We want to avoid him feeling trapped and a sure-fire way to create problems is to allow someone or another animal, to tease your dog while crated.

This may seem a very long-winded way of crating your dog. It's likely you are thinking, 'But I could just shut him in there and he might cry but eventually he will get used to it'.

Some dogs will get over it, and some just suffer in distress quietly; their stress showing up in seemingly unrelated behaviours. Some dogs very obviously don't get over it. They will wreck crates, or physically hurt themselves, or yell their heads off.

A lot of people appear to think a dog screaming and scrabbling to get out of a crate is a dog 'acting out' or a dog who 'needs to get over himself'. That really couldn't be further from the truth. Trapping an animal in a small space is incredibly stressful, if not outright terrifying. Even if your dog never associates that fear with you, it will have a knock-on effect on his ability to learn, settle and generally be a happy, relaxed dog.

I disagree that this is actually all that long-winded. If you are starting out with a puppy, you can get through the first five or six stages in under a week. The later stages would only take longer because a puppy physically can't be left all that long. Frankly, if you don't have a couple of weeks to train a puppy, should you really have taken one on?

It may well take a little longer with an adult dog, but we are talking about five-to-ten-minute sessions to start with, a couple of times a day. It isn't anywhere near the huge undertaking it may seem while reading this through.

The Lounge is for Lounging

How I manage to live in peace with a houseful of crazy Border Collies
By Sally Bradbury

I have several dogs and very few rules, but one that is very strictly upheld is that the lounge is for lounging in.

When we have a puppy, I spend my evenings in the kitchen entertaining the puppy while hubby watches TV with the other dogs in the lounge. We do all our playing and training in the kitchen or outdoors. No toys in the lounge ever.

Over a period of approximately six to ten weeks, I can usually teach a puppy to settle on their bed in the kitchen for an increasing amount of time so that by the time the pup is three to five months old, we can transfer that behaviour to the lounge. Of course, it helps that all the others are setting an example.

In the beginning, I'll be playing, training, teaching some impulse control, doing handling exercises: looking in ears, bit of grooming. This leads to some gentle massage and a settled pup. I might check Facebook on my phone for a minute while the pup is relaxed. A week later, I might be able to reply to an email on my laptop while the pup is quiet on his bed.

We can then go and join the others in the lounge for a few minutes while pup is settled. This is gradually built up, until walking into the lounge becomes the switch to settle.

I would never expect them to do this for longer than they can manage, though. It is built up over several weeks.

Puppy's First Walk

By Sally Bradbury

Everyone looks forward to the day when puppy can go out for a walk for the first time. Exciting times! But what about puppy? Is he as excited as you or is everything overwhelming for him? It's a big scary world out there.

Well before D-day…

Get puppy out and about in your arms or a sling or for car rides. Find somewhere to sit and watch the world go by. Let him see people and dogs and traffic in the distance. Watch for his reactions. Keep him safe;

keep him feeling safe. You really want everything to be a non-event for him. Not too exciting, not overwhelming, and definitely not scary.

People will want to 'ooh' and 'aah' over him. You'll want to show him off, but don't let people overwhelm him. Don't allow strangers to approach him and touch him when he is in your arms unless it is clear that he is happy to make the first move.

Teach puppy to wear a harness and walk nicely on a lead well in advance of wanting to take him for a walk.

There are lots of ways to teach nice lead walking. Here is one suggestion:

At his mealtimes, walk around the house and the garden holding his food bowl. Give him his food one piece at a time from your other hand any time he is there beside you. This is without a lead. Continue to do this until he understands the game and follows you about or walks with you for the whole of his meal.

Meanwhile, use some yummy treats and sit on the floor and get him used to his collar and/or harness. Once he is happy to wear them and sit with his harness on for treats, attach the lead and give him a treat, take it off, give him a treat and so on.

Now, next mealtime, attach the lead to his harness, which he is now fine about. Tuck your end in your belt loop and do as you did before; walking around the house and garden feeding as you go. Voila! Puppy walking on a loose lead.

Keep those early walks with puppy short. Let him stop, take in the view, and have a good sniff. If he can already walk nicely on a lead at home, it pays to continue that lead training in very short bursts outdoors. Puppies don't need lots of road walking. They need to go on little adventures, somewhere where they can safely be on a long line and where they can run and play and explore, then rest and sit and watch the world go by.

Enjoy your walk and make sure puppy does too.

Happy Puppy Care

By Vidhyalakshmi Karthikeyan

Teaching your puppy to enjoy being handled is so important for their welfare.

Puppies will have hundreds of daily interactions with us throughout their lifetime; like having their collar and harness clipped on and off, having their nails done, being brushed, and having small wounds cleaned up and cared for. They are also bound to need to see the vet or receive some medical care at some point.

It is entirely within our ability to make all those experiences wonderful so that our puppies look forward to their everyday maintenance and care for the rest of their lives. Think about never having to worry about giving them a pill or cleaning their ears! Imagine if your adult dog asked to have their nails done instead of hiding when you brought out the clippers! Fear of handling is a thing of the past. The vet and the groomer do not have to be scary places at all.

All of that is possible through carefully structured, highly positive experiences. Every time you clip the collar on, give them a treat. Teach your pup to walk into their harness, rather than you having to push it over them. Leave the clippers out or the ear cleaning solution open as you do other training or just go about your day to allow them to get used to the sights and smells of grooming equipment. Teach your pup that every single time you pick up the clippers, squeezy cheese rains from the tube directly into their mouth. It won't take long before they become excited when they spot you bringing out your nail care equipment!

Ask a friend who visits you to help you teach your pup about handling. Ask them to touch your pup in the places where they already enjoy, usually starting with the shoulders or the chest, and feed your pup as they do so. Ask them to then touch your pup along the back, on the legs or peep into their ears for a second while you continue to associate each of those movements with great treats. Toss some treats away from the two of you for your pup to search and find. Wait for your pup to come back to you for more handling training. Keep it short. Quit while you're ahead.

If your pup hesitates to be touched, he might show it as follows:

- Walking or backing away
- Having ears back
- Showing the whites of his eyes
- Shifting weight back
- Excessive panting
- Pushing your hand away with his muzzle
- Growling or snapping

If any of these behaviours happen, stop, and think why. Take things even slower and teach your pup that your hand simply lifting towards him predicts treats or play.

Also consider how you can break up whatever happened immediately beforehand into much smaller steps and turn that hesitation into optimism, usually by associating those increments with something totally amazing like squeezy cheese or a game of tug.

Husbandry training is vital for a dog. Having a pup is like having a clean slate. The more proactive you can be about teaching them that handling beyond everyday petting is fun and something to look forward to, not just something to be endured until it's over, the better quality of life they will enjoy as adults.

Four on the Floor – Preventing Jumping Up
By Sally Bradbury

To teach a dog to keep four feet on the floor when greeting or just in general, you need at least 30–50 treats per session. The dog's meal, laced with some hot dog sausage is ideal to use. With a piece of food in your hand, approach the dog or let him approach you with your hand at his eye level. Deliver pieces of food in quick succession while the front feet stay firmly planted. Even if just one foot leaves the floor, then the treat is not given until it returns to the floor.

After about 30 repetitions of this, you can start to pause briefly with the food in your hand for just a nanosecond before giving it. The fact that the dog has just had 30 treats with his front feet on floor is going to increase the chances of the dog repeating the same behaviour, except now you are giving the dog a chance to jump, albeit for less than a second.
Feet on floor = treat. Feet leave floor = no treat. Repeat, repeat, repeat.

Gradually start to stand up straighter and wait a bit before giving the treat. A few missed treats for feet leaving the floor (you say nothing by the way, just a quiet 'good' when giving the treat) and your pup will get the message.

So, you teach him the concept of four on the floor first, and then you make a chocolate cake, put some beer in the fridge and invite a few dog-savvy friends over and have them do it, too. You may need a few such sessions, but providing you are consistent, and you use only people who will do as you ask, your dog will soon generalise to all visitors and greet them without jumping on them.

Zoomies
By Abby Huxtable

Zoomies or, to use their official term, Frenetic Random Activity Periods (FRAPs) are well known to most puppy and dog owners.

The official term actually describes them really well – random, frantic activity periods. These periods usually occur after walks, sometimes after meals, and on an evening. They are really common in puppies, as adult dogs often outgrow them, although you do still see the occasional zoomies from adults too.

Not much is scientifically known about zoomies. There have been very few studies on them, so we are unsure what causes them or why they occur. Logically, it is an outlet for excess energy. Marc Berkoff, an American Biologist and Behavioural Ecologist, has written a little on the subject, as have many Dog Trainers/Behaviourists, but no formal studies have been conducted.

The excess energy theory fits with zoomies occurring after walks and on an evening. We restrict our puppy's exercise levels to protect their joints. Walks are also exciting and a bit scary for many puppies, with lots of new sights, smells and sounds each time. Therefore, they have a build-up of energy, which comes out once they get home and are off their leads.

Similarly, the evening is the most common time for zoomies and is the outlet for excess energy left over from the day's activities before they settle down to sleep.

Zoomies take many forms, from running, shaking, and tugging toys, digging, biting at their owners or other animal companions, and humping, just to name a few. They basically consist of whatever activity your dog finds enjoyable as an outlet for energy!

If their chosen outlet is safe for them, you and other residents of your household can simply enjoy the fun. Let them have their zoomies to release their energy, then they will settle and sleep. They may need a chew, Kong, lickimat, or a scatter of food to encourage that settle towards the end of zoomie time.

If, however, the zoomies are dangerous to our dogs or take an unwanted form (usually biting), then we need to channel that energy into other outlets.

This could be simple redirection to a safer area. So, you could let them zoom in the garden rather than the house or cue them to dig a pile of old blankets or their own bed instead of your sofa.

It could also involve setting up activities to have ready for them when you get home from your walk or during their regular zoomie time.

Many enrichment activities can be used for this as they use that energy in mental instead of physical activity and often combine the two.

You could also have a small training or play session with your dog to channel that energy into something more constructive. Do be aware that in zoomie mode, your dog will find it very difficult to listen to you and concentrate, so keep skills simple or engage that energy and attention **before** they hit full zoomie mode!

As our dogs mature and manage their energy levels better, and the world becomes less exciting and scary and more 'normal' to them, zoomies will naturally reduce in frequency. Some dogs lose their zoom totally and some still have occasional, shorter ones. Teaching them how to channel that energy at an early age, will ensure their zoomies are safe and fun for you all, however long they last.

Puppy Confidence
A house of cards? Or a bricks and mortar foundation?
By Emma Judson

While it should be pretty obvious that when we get a new puppy (or a rescue dog that is new to us), their confidence levels will be low. They will be insecure and worried, unsure of how everything works, and they will need comfort from and closeness to us.

Initially, that is going to mean not leaving your puppy (or new rescue dog), giving them constant access to you, and avoiding them experiencing distress. But how do we move on? What is realistic and reasonable to expect?

When we teach our puppies new behaviours, we don't automatically assume that once they sit for the first time when we say 'sit', that the job is done. No, we know that it's going to take more repetitions, more variation, working our way up through a series of variables, such as location, distraction, our body position and probably more.

If it were that easy, dogs would be trained in a matter of minutes and some of us would be out of a job!

But when it comes to confidence, we are often getting things wrong. We assume that after two days in a new home, a puppy will be fine left alone while we work. Why would that be the case? We assume that one night without needing the toilet means puppy can now sleep by themselves rather than in our room or with someone downstairs on the sofa. Why?

A puppy's confidence is initially like a house of cards. You can build a lot quite quickly, but it's shaky. It doesn't take much to knock it over, even if you built it pretty high. In fact, the higher you built it, the more potential there is to knock it down because you have assumed it's more reliable and secure than it really is.

We need to build our puppy's confidence out of bricks and mortar, with solid foundations. So, what does that mean in practical terms?

Look more closely at what you are expecting from your puppy.

If you want him to sleep in a room by himself at night, what skills does he need?

He needs to know what to do by himself. Get a toy, get a drink, settle himself back to sleep, not need the toilet overnight.

He also needs to be able to come and find you to ask to go out. You don't want him screaming his head off to wake you up several rooms and another floor away, so he can't be locked in a pen or crate.

That means you need to trust him to come all the way to find you without weeing or pooing in the hall, chewing the carpet on the stairs, or having a little munch on the bookshelf on the landing.

When you look at your 14-week-old puppy who sleeps by himself next to your bed and hasn't woken up for three nights running, you may think 'yes, he's got this'. But when you look at the above requirements, he still isn't ready, is he?

What happens if we have assumed he *is* ready, and we've popped him downstairs by himself in a pen with his bed?

Let's say he's eaten something dodgy earlier in the day and his tummy wakes him, or he's heard a noise outdoors that he hasn't heard before.

He wakes up, there's no one there, he fidgets about or does a little woof. No one comes, so he does a bigger woof or a howl. It takes him a few minutes of howling to get you to come, and he may have already had a poo-splosion or done a lake of wee before you get there.

You arrive, bleary eyed, frustrated at being woken, annoyed that now you've a mess to clean up. From **his** point of view, he wanted comfort and relief from his predicament. What he has received is his primary caregiver who is exuding 'NOT HAPPY' vibes at him, no matter how much they try to slap on a cheerful voice and deal with him kindly. That's not going to boost his confidence, is it?

It's also going to frustrate and annoy you. He could do this last night; why can't he cope tonight? He's slept through for weeks now; when can you get your sleep back?

Let's look at what would have happened had he still been in your room.

He hears a sound. He wakes. Everyone else is sleeping. He might just assume everyone else is not worried, therefore it's all fine and goes back to sleep.

He has a tummy rumble. It feels worrying. He wakes and woofs. You wake and take him outdoors, bleary eyed and wishing you weren't standing outdoors in the rain in your PJs, but glad to have avoided the poonami that is now coming out of your puppy.

He's learned that if he needs help, it's there. Hurrah!

But what other reasons are there for your puppy's confidence to wax and wane?

Quite simply, they are a puppy. They are constantly learning and constantly growing. It takes a toll, both physically and mentally.

This happens to you, too. Even once you are an adult. Imagine you've just taken on a new job or are learning a new skill. For a while, you improve each day and feel great. After a while, you suddenly realise the vast chasm between where you are now and where you need to be, and it feels daunting. And you have a wobble.

While puppies don't know how much it is they have yet to learn, they can still be overwhelmed at times. They have to cope with all the new information they are learning, the physical fatigue that comes from growing, and the experiences they have to process, both good and bad. Sometimes the system has a bit of a crash. Instead of our brave, confident, possibly bolshy puppy, we have a snuggly, needy puppy, who wants to cuddle into our bodies, and can't sleep without being wedged into our arms or under our chins.

If your puppy is in your room, and if you are making yourself available to your puppy as they grow, then this isn't a big deal.

If you have leapt ahead and assumed the confidence and progress achieved is permanent, however, then there can be a big problem. If your puppy needs you and you are not available, hello major drama and distress.

Furthermore, there is a deep sense somewhere within the human species that coping with distress is somehow good for us. I don't really think it is. **I think the saying 'what doesn't kill us makes us stronger' is rubbish. What doesn't kill us often damages us and the way we process events in the future.** It's certainly turned me into a suspicious and cynical person at times!

There are **no** benefits to your puppy experiencing distress. It will not teach them to cope. It will not help them 'get over it'. It will simply damage the way they learn and grow. Avoid it, at pretty much all costs.

I would bet that by now some people are saying, 'but when do I know my puppy's confidence is real and is reasonably unshakeable, and I can progress in teaching things like sleeping alone and being left alone when I go to the shops?'

It's always going to be an educated guess. So, the answer is to do things gradually and test things out before you do them for real.

If you think your puppy can cope when you nip to the shops for ten minutes, test it out by going and sitting in your car for ten minutes while watching your puppy on a camera. That way, if you are wrong, you can return **before** your puppy has a horrible distressing crisis.

We can also help our puppies along by setting up games and training sessions that reward independence. Also, by accurately observing and keeping notes or diaries on our puppy's progress.

When we see our puppy happily take themselves off out of the noisy living room to snooze in the quiet kitchen; hurrah! That's a good sign our puppy can make decisions by himself.

When we see our puppy take his chew toy and trot off into the garden to enjoy it outdoors without us; brilliant!

When we are busy flitting about doing the ironing or tidying up and our puppy sighs and heaves himself up and out to chew his toy in his bed in the living room because we are being annoying and disturbing his sleep; fantastic!

Also note the things our puppy does when we return from upstairs or out in the garden. Are we greeted with dramatic displays of joy that we have safely returned from Mordor, where we were almost certain to die? Or are we greeted with a casual, 'oh, you're back, nice, I'm busy' and our puppy looks up and then returns to sleep or returns to whatever they were doing.

Make it a habit to keep notes or diaries on what your puppy does. What he experiences and how he reacts will help you make these educated guesses as to what he is really ready for.

It is safer to test things out a few times before doing something 'for real', where you may be delayed or unable to drop everything and return. This means you are much less likely to make a mistake and push your puppy too far, too soon.

Finally, keep in mind that we are under constant social pressure to form expectations that are NOT realistic for our puppies. We have to work hard to be reasonable and squash that.

We may want to get a puppy and then go back to work in a week. That's not realistic. That's going to cause the puppy distress unless we can make a compromise. Take time off, get a dog sitter or daycare, whatever.

We may prefer not to have a dog in our bedroom full-time, and that's fine. However, it is likely to take you nearer a year to get there than a couple of weeks.

We can put in all the preparation work and foundation building we like, but we can only ever go at the pace our puppy is capable of going at. Remember, this is a marathon and not a sprint. You have 12 to 15, or even more, years with your puppy. The reality is that you do not need to get all of this stuff done in the first month or two of your puppy's life with you. If you really, really do, then perhaps a puppy is not for you at the moment!

Taking things slow and steady might seem tough. In fact, progress is often *easier* if you go slowly. You can manage frustration, stress, and sleep better if you don't rush.

Fear Periods
Or why the heck? This was fine yesterday?!
By Emma Judson

You have probably heard about fear periods in puppy development. At certain points in a puppy's progression from tiny baby to bold, confident adult dog, they will experience fear of things or situations.

The first fear period occurs from around eight weeks to 16 weeks. For some puppies, it won't begin until nearer 16 weeks. For others, it hits at eight weeks. They suddenly find that the world contains potentially dangerous, scary things, and this helps to temper their previous confident, happy-go-lucky natures. It's nature's way of stopping them being stomped on by a mammoth or eaten by a sabre-toothed cat.

Later on, however, they will experience a second fear period, or at least most of them will. Not all pups do. This stage is much less clearly defined. Depending on what you read, you might be expecting a couple of weeks where your now nearly grown-up dog is a bit wimpy about stuff. Then it will all be over and everything will be fine.

Unfortunately, this isn't the case!

The secondary fear period may start as early as six months or as late as 18 months. It is tied in with adolescence and the hormones that increase, drop, fluctuate, whizz round, switch off ears, switch on noses (and other body parts), and turn your puppy from saint to sinner; from sweetheart to total rotter!

Those hormones are pushing your dog to try out new behaviour, to push boundaries and to find out 'what happens if'. They're causing your dog to struggle to listen to you, to forget previously familiar lessons or behaviours, and they can result in a gung-ho, 'you can't make me' attitude. In some dogs, particularly in boys, it can result in an 'OK then, challenge me, just try it!' combative attitude. A dollop of fear could help to rein that in.

But in some cases, it doesn't. It can actually make matters worse. Instead of a healthy spot of wariness or caution, we see dogs who are flat-out terrified of something that was fine the day before; dogs who are pushed by their fear to confront and behave aggressively, whether that is a bluff or not. This doesn't seem like a useful evolutionary function to me.

I believe the second fear stage has lost its relevance. It no longer determines whether an animal stays safe so that they can reproduce or not. We're keeping our dogs safe, and we aren't deciding who breeds and who doesn't based on any link to this fear stage. We are seeing the effects of dogs with abnormal or non-existent fear stages reproducing. In the wild, they would not survive to do so.

We can also see that the manifestations of aggression have been adapted through selective breeding; animals with modified behaviour sequences such as collies, who eye – stalk – chase, but do not grab/bite/kill/dissect, or pointers who just go from eye to freeze (their 'stalk' mode being modified into the point position). So we have changed a lot of the behaviours dogs naturally perform, and how they think.

With this in mind, it makes sense that this secondary fear period is so vague as to when it occurs, what behaviours it may trigger, and how long it lasts.

For some pups, there will be a clear change. They may suddenly be more needy and clingy, back off from strangers or even folk they know, or start barking and clearly looking worried.

For some, that breeding will mean they don't back off. They'll keep approaching, but instead of your soft, wiggly puppy, you've got a stiff, shaking, hackles-up pup, erupting into a volley of angry sounding barks.

The pups who are visibly scared will fare quite well. As long as they're looked after, the fear won't escalate. Instead, they will be removed from scary situations and taken off to do something nice. They'll be OK.

The pups who look confident may not be. These are the ones who are more likely to be mistaken for truly confident, or rude, or aggressive, or plain 'bad'. They may well not be OK.

Fear cannot be reduced by force. The old adage 'face your fears' is a human construct. In reality, it doesn't actually work all that well for people much of the time.

For 20 years, I forced myself to do something I found scary. The thing was rewarding to do (I got paid!), nothing truly awful ever happened. In fact, only once did something slightly unpleasant occur. I felt huge relief after the event, every time. I willingly put myself up to do it again, but that fear did not go away. I remain as anxious and fearful of it as I was 20 years ago.

So what can we do to mitigate fear periods?

- Avoid the scary stuff
- Use tasty treats to reinforce mildly worrying situations
- Be kind. Reduce stress in every area you can think of
- Go back to basics. Instead of pushing for progress, recover old ground at an easier level
- This too shall pass. Go home, stay there, just play games and have fun
- Listen to your pup. Believe them if they say they are unhappy

Some of these things are so simple. Stay at home if your pup looks a bit wimpy or needy. That's never hard to do.

Some of them may be much harder, particularly if your puppy is of the brave 'take-on-the-world-and-bite-its-ass' type, and not the 'meep-from-behind-the-sofa' type. Watch your puppy and truly listen to what they are telling you.

The hardest part is other people. If your puppy says that Uncle Kevin is now a scary puppy eating monster and Aunty Mary is, in fact, Cruella DeVille and wants to make a puppy fur coat, it can be hard to explain to them why they can't fuss your dog or why they can't come round for tea this week.

You need to be prepared to be potentially rude to people; to tell them 'no'. Back off. Go away. Relatives, friends, strangers, if your puppy says 'no', then you need to advocate for them.

It would be wonderful if we could promise that a fear stage will last just a week or so and be done with. The reality is that for some, it will be a few days here, a few days there, on and off for months. Be ready to go with the flow!

It really will get better. With patience, kindness and quite a lot of sausage, you and your pup will get there in the end.

Chapter 3

Separation Anxiety or Frustration

Preventing Separation-Related Anxiety or Frustration

Written during the 2020/21 Covid-19 Pandemic.
By Emma Judson

Currently, we are all supposed to be staying at home, going out as little as possible, and it is tempting to think that this is brilliant news for our dogs.

And it might be... But!

For some dogs, that change in routine is going to be stressful. Even if it's fun, it might still be adding stress.

It may also cause a breakdown in routine. When you return to work and to socialising outside your house without your dog, you could face a significant problem. Your dog can no longer cope with being left.

So, what can you do?

Manage Stress, Reduce Stress, Avoid Stress

These should be your first steps when addressing any change in routine or trying to change behaviour.

Observe your dog. What winds them up? What worries them? What sends them giddy? Take some notes and then either avoid those things, or sandwich them between more calming, relaxing activities.

Example: Watching wildlife out of the window sends my terrier loopy. He can't get at it. He'd like to chase it, but he cannot, so he yells and it runs away. That's reinforced his behaviour, so he repeats it and gets himself into a right state.

Solution: Block his view by using frosted window film. Move furniture. Draw blinds. Entertain him in another room. This breaks that cycle of stress, reinforcement, more stress.

Example: My partner is in another room that dogs do not usually go in. The door is shut, and he can be heard shouting at computer games. The dogs find this really frustrating as they cannot get to him. They become anxious because of the loud sounds.

Solution: Turn down the volume. Entertain the dogs in another room with something calming. Suggest partner plays different games or does not play. Suggest that dogs be allowed in the room with him so they can see what's going on/be with him.

By noting down what winds up and upsets the dog, and then finding workarounds, you can reduce stress quite a lot. For the things you can't avoid, try giving your dogs a calming activity such as Free Work, scent games, massage, or simply finding scattered food to bring them back down. Remember, not all dogs find the same thing relaxing!

OK, So Now What?
My dog is now calm, my house is a serene haven of chill…

If you had a routine of leaving your dog before the Covid-19 lockdown, and your dog was genuinely OK with that, then approximate that routine as much as you can.

For example, if you got up at eight o'clock, dressed and went out, then get up at eight o'clock, dress and go read your emails in your car.

By sticking to as much of the routine as is practical, the change when you do go back to work will be minimised and your dog will tolerate it far better.

Again, make notes as to what your routine is. What actions or events are significant to your dog?

If your dog thinks that you putting on work shoes and lippy is significant, then include that in your routine. If he thinks you putting on your PJs and slippers means you are staying home, then do not use those to go and sit in the car. It won't meet his idea of a normal routine.

If your dog was **not** OK with being left pre-lockdown and they already had a problem with separation, then **do not** follow the instructions above. You will simply cause frustration and distress.

For the dogs and puppies who have not yet been left, you will first need to desensitise them to all the potential triggers that will eventually tell them that you are leaving. Then gradually build up an 'absence routine'.

The key point is that you avoid frustration or anxiety. Identify all the possible triggers in list form and keep adding and amending that list. Keep diaries on what your dog has seen, done, experienced, and how they have slept each day. Break each stage down into tiny steps – tinier than you may think possible or necessary!

Example: Bert starts to worry when his owner puts on her work shoes, starts filling her handbag with stuff, looking for keys, and putting on her coat.

To desensitise Bert, we identify that work shoes, handbag, looking for stuff, keys and coat are all triggers.

Then we take **one** of the triggers from this list, let's say handbag.

- Pick up handbag, put handbag down immediately
- Repeat five times without speaking to Bert, but keeping an eye on him
- If he settles while this is going on, we know that's OK. If Bert does not settle or if Bert gets more worried, we know this is too much so we will refine further

Bert doesn't settle, but doesn't get worse.

- So, now the new routine is to touch the handbag but **not** pick it up, five times in a row
- Bert settles while this happens
- When Bert reliably settles during this desensitisation session, and when his face says 'meh, I don't care about this', we know we can add something else. We can push the desensitisation a little further.
- So, now the new routine we try is to touch the handbag five times and lift it, but not fully pick it right up just once within those five repetitions
- Touch, touch, touch and lift, touch, touch, end

The same sort of break-down applies to all those potential triggers. Start at a point where you think Bert will be OK. Watch carefully and if he is not OK, scale it down. If he *is* OK with it, you can push things a little further.

Always be ready to drop back a bit on the difficulty or duration of a session, even if the dog is doing well. Even when it looks like nothing is happening, the dog is processing what's going on. If we simply make things harder and harder, we will go too far, and cause a plateau or a backslide in progress.

Eventually, you should have a whole list of triggers that are now, at least in some contexts, no longer triggers. Hurrah!

Now you go back through the process, but this time adding the triggers together. Mix this up in different combinations: shoes and bag; coat and keys; bag and keys; bag and coat. Then try to add in three things, or four things, and so on.

This does sound very tedious, complicated, and chaotic, which is why you really do need to keep good notes of what you are doing and how he is dealing with it.

Finally: we do not use food to desensitise. Food creates arousal and that's stressful. So, wherever possible, we don't use food.

If you cannot break a trigger down into a small enough step to achieve desensitisation, if your dog is still fearful or worried, and that either gets worse or doesn't improve, then use food to counter-condition first.

So, that would look like this:

- Touch bag. Give treat. Repeat five times. End
- Touch bag. Touch bag. Give treat. Repeat three times. End
- Touch bag. Give treat. Touch bag. Give treat. End

Sometimes we give a treat every time and sometimes we don't, but we make the session shorter. Mixing things up like this can reduce the arousal a little. If you have a frustrated dog, then do less, make it easier, or even reduce the value of your treats.

The goal here is that your dog sees the trigger and gets his 'woohoo treat time' face on. This, of course, means that once we have changed his emotional response from 'argh, scary!' to 'woohoo, yay', we **still** need to desensitise to get back down from 'woohoo yay' to 'meh, I don't care'.

Building desensitisation routines and building absence routines are tricky things to do. I strongly recommend you find a separation anxiety practitioner to help guide and support you through that process. If not, it can become too overwhelming, too difficult to see progress, and very easy to get wrong or give up!

Can't I Just Shut my Dog in Another Room for a Few Hours
while I get on with work? Won't that help him stay used to being alone?

I have seen this recommendation elsewhere and it really makes me cringe.

If your dog is already OK with being left shut in another room or shut out of the room you are in while you are home, then fine. That's not a problem and it won't cause problems. However, it will not prepare him for you being out of the house. He knows you are home!

You really cannot trick a dog into thinking you are out when you are in. He can smell you; he can hear you; he can feel you walking around. The air around your house moves differently with various doors shut/open.

If your dog is already not OK with this, if it causes him to bark or whine or shred the carpet or chew stuff, he won't become OK with it by magic. It will not help him when you go back to work, either.

What if I Distract him with a Kong or Chew?

Nope. Distraction, if done successfully, means your dog doesn't know whether you are out or at home. So, he isn't learning how to cope with that, he's too busy. He hasn't learned anything.

It can also be unsuccessful.

Your dog may learn that the Kong or the chew predicts something unpleasant happening, and so begins to show anxiety when you start to prepare the Kong or hand over the chew.

Your dog may be successfully distracted, but if he finishes his chew or toy before you return, he may suddenly discover he is alone and panic or become very anxious.

Your dog may find trying to destuff a Kong very frustrating. I see this quite a lot as people go to ever greater lengths to make the Kong hard to de-stuff. So, he is more likely to bark, dig, whine, howl, or indeed, just give up and be very upset.

Your dog may be too distressed to be distracted by the toy. I see this a lot as well. In some cases, the presence of a delicious Kong they cannot currently eat simply adds to the anxiety and frustration of the situation! If you have ever sat at your desk with your lunch on a plate, but have been too busy to eat it, you will have some understanding of how that feels!

So, What Can I Do?

Aside from what I have already mentioned, you can play games that encourage independence, help him choose to go (and stay) away from you, and that build confidence.

Simple games that involve your dog going away to find food or toys are easy to devise and can really reinforce that it is safe to do this.

You can also allow your dog (particularly new rescue dogs and puppies) as much contact with you as they want, as this builds security. The more secure and confident they are, the easier it is to teach them and the better their capacity for tolerating things they'd rather not do later on!

Getting Puppy or New Dog Used to Being Alone
Where's Your Dinner Game
By Emma Judson

This game is an easy and simple way to build a bit of independence and confidence in a puppy or a new dog. It is based on free choice on the dog's part and can be adapted in any number of ways as their confidence builds.

It requires two people and a bowl of food!

1. One person holds the puppy at one end of the room while the other places their bowl of food down at the far end of the room, and then quickly returns to the puppy.
2. Puppy is quickly released (this is not about teaching a wait!) to go and find their food, which is easy to do as they can see it!
3. Humans stay put where the puppy left them!

The puppy now chooses to go away from her humans, to get to her food. She is rewarded for making this choice by getting her bowl of food. If she turns to look, or chooses to return, her people are exactly where she left them. This builds confidence and trust, and it's simple to do.

To adapt this game, as your puppy gets bolder, you can now pop the bowl down just out of sight. Around the corner of the sofa or just around an open doorway. The aim now is that puppy has their head out of sight as they eat. They can still check back and see you, or return to you at any point.

If your puppy does check back, that's fine. If they check, come away from a full bowl to find you, and do not return quickly to eat the rest of their meal, then scale the game back so it's a bit easier again for a few days.

Once your puppy can put their head out of sight of you and eat, the next step is to put the bowl where the puppy must go completely out of sight. Again, the same rules apply. You stay still. If puppy checks and carries on eating, that's fine. If they come back to you and won't go finish their meal, you need to scale back.

Eventually, you should be able to have your puppy go and find their bowl around the house, eat the meal at a normal pace (you might want to use pet cameras in the early stages!) and come back to find you. If they are still toilet training, you may want one of the people playing the game to go find the puppy as they finish to prevent any accidents!

Now you can adapt the game further to include treats, toys, food dispensing puzzles, and various rooms upstairs or out in the garden.

Eventually, you can add a cue such as 'find it' to this game and use it on walks to find family members in a game of hide and seek or to find hidden toys or patches of scattered treats.

This game, and *The Flitting Game*, are the preparatory stages for building your dog's confidence and sense of security. Together with careful management and avoiding leaving your dog alone before they can cope, these are the foundations for preventing separation anxiety related problems.

The Flitting Game
By Emma Judson

There's a two-part game that I call *The Flitting Game*. To play, start off by choosing two adjacent rooms, ideally the kitchen and living room.

Set the timer on your phone (silently) for five minutes, then make multiple trips from one room to the next; fiddle with something in one room, and then move on. As you do this, ignore your dog. As in, don't talk to him or touch him but keep an eye on him. When he begins to settle, flit again.

Over the course of a few sessions, you should find your dog becomes slower to get up, slower to settle, lurks in the hallway or in doorways, and starts to look annoyed at you because this is now tedious. Ugh! And unrewarding.

It's important to remember that this is not some strict military regime. If you want your dog to come with you, to talk to him, to fuss him, fine. You can invite him along outside of these sessions.

The point is, when you do not invite him, it might not be worth his effort to follow you. Once he has realised that, you can occasionally add in a good reason to choose not to follow you.

So, step two is to add that reason. A big juicy bone, a big, filled Kong, something that's highly rewarding and a pain in the backside to lift and carry around.

Now repeat the flitting. If he chooses not to follow you, try to spend a little less time in the 'away' room, a little more in the 'home' room, and build up gradually, second by second.

Don't always give the Kong or bone, continue doing sessions without; very gradually build up to other rooms and longer durations away.

At any point, your dog is free to come and check that you're still there. If he does, that's fine. Don't say hi or anything, but make a mental note that perhaps this was a step too far and so scale back.

The idea is that your dog learns that it's his choice not to follow and that sometimes, that choice is highly reinforcing. At other times, it's just saving him some tedium and effort. He is free to check up if he's worried. There's no force or pressure at all.

Hatting
Or the creation of a visual cue that tells your dog you are currently unavailable, regardless of whether present or absent
By Emma Judson

For some dogs, we need a way to tell them that we aren't available. We are boring and uninteresting, and therefore there is no point bothering us.

This can be useful for dogs with separation anxiety and for dogs who need to learn to calm down in the house due to previously learned attention-seeking behaviours*.

---

* Attention-seeking behaviour should be taken seriously and not treated as if the dog is bad or wrong. Dogs seeking attention are dogs that are either not getting the right amount of attention or the right kind of attention!

Dogs form associations between visual cues and our behaviour all the time. They are doing it constantly and this is how they know what's going to happen before it does. It's why they get excited about a walk when you have simply walked to the hook where the lead is kept, or start the dinner dance when you close your laptop, say 'right then', and head to the kitchen.

We can, if we are careful and clever about it, use this to our advantage!

Find a hat or a scarf. You can use other items, like a traffic cone on the coffee table or a beachball hung off the light fittings, but a hat or scarf is convenient, cheap, and portable. Choose one that fits the following criteria:

- Your dog has never seen it before
- It is of a colour they can actually perceive
- It changes your outline slightly, so they are aware of the difference between you wearing it and not wearing it
- They are not scared of it

The rules of 'hatting' are as follows:

- When you wear the hat, there is no dog. No eye contact, no talk, no touch**
- Hat goes on and off without any link to dog's behaviour
- If your dog has some sort of urgent need, you must remove hat and deal with dogs need in a way that looks like the two events are not related, so the dog never thinks you stopped hatting as a result of his or her behaviour

Ideally, you will already have spotted some sedentary, or at least stationary, behaviour of yours that your dog tends to assume means you aren't available for attention. You can then use this to introduce hatting. Things like ironing, playing on your phone, or using the computer will often meet this criterion.

If you already have something like that, simply wear the hat while you do it and remember to remove the hat before you finish doing whatever it is.

If you do not have such a set up already, or can't identify one, the best thing to do is hat while reading a magazine (so your hands are occupied,

---

** You are not really ignoring your dog; he just thinks you are. This is not about ignoring a dog's genuine need or distress. Ever.

and you are clearly doing something). Do not hat by sitting and staring into space, as your dog will find that weird and creepy, and possibly be a bit upset!

The goal is that when you hat, your dog does not try to get your attention, and gradually learns he cannot get attention from you without ever really needing to. This should look like nothing is really happening in the initial stages.

Very occasionally, you'll get a dog who will try to get your attention (most likely in attention-seekers rather than separation anxiety cases). As long as you are not building frustration or distress by ignoring, carry on. If you think there is the slightest chance you are building frustration or distress, stop. Time sessions for a shorter duration, and re-evaluate the rest of your dog's training protocol. There's the possibility that this method is not suitable for your dog right now.

Once you get past the initial stages, and you think your dog has grasped that you wearing the hat means that you are unavailable, you can start to add in other hatting situations. If you are at this stage, you should have a relaxed dog who has taken himself off to do his own thing; sleep, chew a toy or do something similar. So, if you initially hatted while on the laptop, you may now try hatting while watching TV, or hatting while ironing, or hatting while reading a book in the kitchen.

Gradually add more hatting situations or increase the duration, but don't do both at once. Take it steady!

When your dog sees you start to hat, clearly understands, and takes themselves off to get comfy no matter where or when you hat, you can start to hat while doing some other element of your training programme.

For example, if you play *The Flittling Game*, you might hat and flit. If you are desensitizing to leaving triggers, you might hat and fiddle with keys or a coat or shoes.

Hatting can be very good for dogs who assume that when you go out, they are missing out on a fun trip. It's also great for dogs who are still able to see you once you've left your property, for instance from a door or window as you walk along the street. Once they understand that hat = no attention/this activity is not for you, it transfers quite well to you leaving. You were unavailable anyway, so there's no cause for frustration!

It rarely works all by itself, however, so you will have to work on absence duration, desensitisation, or counter-conditioning to leaving triggers, as well as hatting, but it can be a useful tool in your toolkit!

The Hokey Cokey Game
By Emma Judson

This game is designed to counter-condition dogs to the sometimes innately unpleasant experience of group members leaving the group (or the dog plus a human having to leave the group).

Dogs are pretty much pre-programmed to want groups to stay together. This includes groups of people or dogs they know, like family at home, and groups they don't know so well, like a bunch of people who met up for a walk, as well as groups of animals, like sheep or cattle.

We took this desire to keep a group together and selectively bred for it in some dogs, hence cattle dogs, sheep dogs, herding dogs, and droving dogs. Some want to keep the group in one place (German Shepherds), some want to bring the group to you (Border Collies), some want to take the group somewhere else (Bearded Collies, Cattle Dogs), but *none* of them want the group to split up or disperse out of their sight!

Even if your dog is not a herding or droving breed, they still have a desire to keep their social group together, and are still likely to find it upsetting if that group splits up.

So, if your dog has an issue with someone wanting to nip into the coffee shop or newsagents on your walk, if they can't handle it when you are at a café and someone goes inside to order or to use the loo – that's why.

This game helps make someone leaving or being removed from the group a good thing, rather than a bad thing.

You'll need:

- At least two people
- Treats or a tug toy that your dog likes
- Your dog
- Some space
- Good communication skills

Things you can vary later:

- How many people
- Who leaves
- Whether they go out of sight or not
- Whether they leave or the dog leaves
- The amount of the reward
- What the reward is
- Location
- Level of distraction in the environment.

As always, it's recommended to start out easy:

- Fewer people
- Home environment
- People stay in sight
- Reward value is high
- When you alter something, just alter one thing at a time
- As you progress through the levels of difficulty, it may be wise to make some of the variables easier

How to play:

- Agree beforehand how you will tell the 'leaver' when to stop or return, or how they will work this out.
- I'd recommend starting with one step and repeating that a few times
- Then two steps
- Avoid anything obvious, like them moving away a few steps and shouting back, 'Now? Is this far enough? How about now?', or them continuing to go too far and you shrieking, 'No that's too far! Come back!'
- They step out and *as* they arrive at that one step away (or two steps or three steps), you reward your dog
- Once the reward is consumed, they come back to the start point

That's it, really. When one step is OK, chuck in two, dip back down to one sometimes, work your way to three, dip back down to one or two from time to time, add in a fourth, and so on.

When the game is understood and enjoyed, start altering variables one at a time. You might be at ten steps, and you decide that now it's time to go from the living room to the back garden. When you do, that environment will be a little tougher. So, start back out at, say, two steps, and work back up to ten. It shouldn't take long.

Proceed this way for as many steps as you need. Work out in advance which elements your dog will find hardest and work on the easy things first!

Alternatively, you could work on the dog leaving. While this is less likely to be something that your dog has a problem with, it's still worth doing to ensure that they really are fine. It is easier, as the person who has the dog oversees how far and when to reward. You only need the other group members to stay put and stay quiet!

Things to avoid:

- Don't push your dog too far, too fast. It's way better to stop when your dog is still loving this game than to push for 'just one more step' and trigger anxiety or stress
- Don't rush to phase out food. Yes, we do need to in the end, but no, it doesn't have to be this minute!
- **Do not** reward your dog as the person starts to return or as they arrive back. They are already being rewarded for that by the person arriving back. We want to make them **being away** very rewarding. We don't want to make their return more rewarding than it already is!
- Do not use the food to distract your dog as the person is leaving either!

Alone Training – The Next Steps
By Abby Huxtable

Many people assume that once crate trained, their puppy or dog will be OK alone. While crate training can help set your dog up to be OK alone, it is unfortunately not enough.

Yes, your dog has learnt to love their crate – *but* they have learnt to do so while you are there. You haven't actually taught them to be OK in the crate while you are not there.

You also may not wish to crate your dog. You may wish them to be in a certain area, such as a pen or a room, or you may be happy to leave them with the run of the house. Any one of these options is fine, as long as it suits the dog and your family, and is safe.

So, *how* do we teach our dogs to be OK alone?

Hopefully, you have been playing *The Flitting Game*, and have also been working on making a crate, pen, bed, or room valuable to your dogs. Basically, wherever you plan on them being when you do leave them.

If you have done all of this, your dog will have built up their confidence in being able to be away from you within the home. Be aware that some dogs just like to be with you when you are home. This doesn't necessarily mean they will struggle when you are gone, but if they *can* be alone when you are there, you being gone will be less of a challenge for them.

Make sure your dog isn't hungry or thirsty, has had some exercise, and is ready to settle or knows how to settle in their area.

We don't need treats in any of this, as the aim is 'oh, whatever'. It is all desensitisation training.

Therefore, when you are flitting, start to pop out through the external doors and straight back in.

Add the barrier to their area, either the crate door, room door, or baby gate, so you pop out and they remain within, you pop back in again. You may need to do this in stages. So, shut the barrier a quarter of the way, then, when pup is OK with that, shut it halfway, then three quarters of the way, then lean the door shut, and finally shut it properly.

As you increase the duration of this, you can also add popping through the external door and straight back in.

Slowly build up the duration of these absences. Try to do it in a non-linear fashion and always ensure you return BEFORE any signs of distress. If your dog never experiences distress at being left, they will never know to be distressed by you leaving them.

Signs of distress can be:

- Howling
- Barking
- Crying
- Destructive behaviours
- Toileting
- Scratching at barriers

There are also more subtle ones:

- Yawning
- Lip licking
- Scratching themselves
- Dejected body language (looking sad/worried)
- Avoiding their area
- Being reluctant to leave you

A relaxed dog has loose body language, settles comfortably, will change position, and relax, may move around but re-settles easily, and does not look for the exits as he is happy in his area. Such a dog will have a relaxed drink, may play, or eat, and then easily re-settles.

Technology is a brilliant tool here. A decent pet camera can be bought for as little as £25; better ones can be slightly more expensive. You can set up a video call between two devices, or at least record your dog while you are out. Obviously, the recording cannot tell you live information, though, to enable you to return if need be.

It is also good to desensitise to your leaving cues. In plain English, make a list of everything you do before you leave, for example:

- Put your dog in their area
- Give them a treat
- Put your shoes on
- Get your keys
- Get your wallet/bag
- Put your coat on
- Check the doors are locked
- Check the mirror
- Toilet

Then randomly do these things when you are not leaving. Your dog then does not know they are the cues for you to be leaving them, they are just things that happen throughout the day. A handy way of doing this is by making a check list and ticking off when you do a couple of them.

Aim to tick off two or three cues each day, a couple of times each. For example, pick up your keys, wander about with them or go sit on your sofa. Then put them back. Same with your shoes or coat. Do a couple more the next day, and so on. Mix it up, so again, it's random. Then when your dog doesn't bat an eyelid at any of those, start to combine a couple of them, again, without leaving.

Then sometimes do a couple and pop out and back in.

Then another couple but don't leave.

Then a different two and pop out for a bit longer (if your dog is OK with this).

Keep building the cues and the duration slowly, always making sure to return **before** any distress.

All of this sounds like a lot – you might start to feel as if you are going to be stuck at home for weeks!

Not true. If you have been laying the foundations of the flitting combined with a valuable area of their own, these last few stages can progress very quickly. Each of the sessions are seconds and minutes in length – not hours. You can easily complete them throughout the day and do them often.

As long as your dog remains calm and chilled, you will be able to increase the duration pretty quickly, too.

NOTE: we would never recommend leaving dogs for longer than four hours without some sort of break. Younger dogs can only be left for shorter periods of time, as they cannot hold their bladders that long, which will cause distress in itself.

Doorway to... Enlightenment?

By Emma Judson

Doors are a big deal for dogs. Part of almost every dog's separation related behaviour modification programme is likely to involve desensitising your dog to human activity around doors, like exiting, entering, opening, closing, and locking.

But let's think about *why* doors are such a big deal for most dogs.

Your front door:

- People come in (*Woohoo* or *argh scary!*)
- People leave (*Eek!*)
- People knock on it (*Startling, exciting, worrying?*)
- People shove things through it (*Fun, scary?*)
- Humans dash to the door when people knock on it or shove things through it
- Walks happen via the door
- People dash through the door and shut it quickly in the dog's face to prevent escape
- People slam doors

Some of this applies to internal doors, too. Both slamming and slipping through them quickly, then shutting them to prevent the dog getting through, are pretty common events.

Barriers that a dog cannot see through can increase frustration, but so can barriers that a dog *can* see through. For example, a glazed door with a view of a busy garden full of cats or a busy street can also build frustration.

Most of the things that build arousal, frustration, anxiety, and excitement around doors don't actually *need* to happen!

They happen because we haven't really thought about it, we slip into bad habits, or we assume that's just the way it is.

It is easy to change some of these things though:

- Stick a note on your door telling people you will be slow to answer
- Stop rushing to the door

- Disconnect the bell and put a note saying DO NOT KNOCK, and your phone number
- Put a mailbox on the outside of the house so that the postal delivery doesn't mean letters are shoved through the door
- If you have the choice of accessing your home through a front and a back door, pick one door that the dog leaves through, and one door that you leave through without the dog
- If your dog never goes for walks through the front door and that's the door you leave through to go out, he will not assume he's missing a walk, because that door does not lead to walks!
- Retrain your dog (by using a new bell) so that the sound of the bell becomes a cue to get in his bed for a treat. Only attach the new bell to the door once that behaviour is rock solid

Once we think about it, there is much we can do to reduce the stress that doors cause. The more stress we can reduce, the more capacity your dog has to cope with the stress we can't reduce.

Chapter 4

Anxious and Fearful Dogs

Calming Products and Anxiety Medications

By Jo Maisey

Chronic stress can cause serious medical problems in dogs, including weakened immune systems, digestive diseases, and heart disease. Acute stress can *sensitise* dogs to environments and people, thus creating a more negative association than before, and potentially causing behavioural problems to escalate.

There are a variety of products and protocols that *may* help *some* dogs. It would be a case of trial and error. I would suggest that none of them will have enough of an effect to be able to help a truly phobic dog. Plus, while you play around trying to find something that *may* help, your dog is going through an incredibly stressful time.

Some of these products or protocols are as follows:

- Thundershirt
- Adaptil. Available as a collar, spray or plug in
- Karen Overall's Relaxation Protocol. Also available as MP3 files
- Zylkene
- Tellington TTouch
- Bach Flowers Rescue Remedy
- Skullcap and Valerian
- Pet Remedy
- L-theanine

NOTE: Just because something is 'herbal' or 'natural' does not necessarily mean it is safe for your dog. It is always best to check with your vet before proceeding. Many over the counter (OTC) products are untested, unproven, and expensive.

There are many tried and tested medications for fear or anxiety, which can only be prescribed by a qualified and licensed vet. Your vet should know your dog's medical history and chat through the various options. For fearful dogs, the clock is ticking. While you trial any of the above, your dog may be getting worse. Noise phobias, such as thunderstorms and fireworks, can worsen.

Various medications are available for different types of phobias. Some are for generalised fear and anxiety, some are for situational fear, such as vet visits, thunder, or fireworks, some are for separation anxiety, and so on. For some reason, there seems to be a general aversion to using them. Meanwhile, your dog is having an extremely tough time.

NOTE: None of the above will work in isolation. They should all be used alongside a behavioural modification programme.

Working with Fear Issues
By Leah Roberts

Aggression is almost always a fear issue. When we feel threatened, it triggers a fight, flight, or freeze response. Dogs have similar ways of responding to threat. They may hide behind something and shake, lunge and attack, or just freeze on the spot. In all cases, you want to address the underlying fear, not the behaviour. Once you have healed the fear, the behaviour will change on its own.

There are two methods of dealing with fear that work beautifully. Both are ways of associating good things with the trigger (object of fear) and changing the perception that the trigger is threatening.

Open Bar/Closed Bar
As long as the trigger is in sight, chicken (or a very special yummy treat) is being shovelled into the dog's mouth. I also like to 'cheerlead', that is, praise in a happy tone of voice. When the trigger moves out of sight, the chicken and cheering stop.

Click the Trigger
Watch the dog's eyes. As soon as the dog looks at the trigger, click (or use a verbal marker) and immediately hold the chicken to the side of the dog's nose, so that his eye contact is immediately broken to take the treat. Repeat. Repeat.

In both cases, it is *extremely important* to start at a distance or level of intensity where your dog notices the trigger but is not bothered by it. If he's already reacting, you are too close. In both cases, you are working toward getting a 'yay, there's the trigger' reaction. Not just tolerance, but happy excitement. Once you get that, you move a teensy bit closer and start again.

If even once during the therapy your dog is placed over threshold (where he feels threatened), you have lost your progress. So, you may have to change your routine. If you normally walk your dog where there are other dogs who are too close for comfort, walk elsewhere for a while until your dog is fine with that level of intensity. If you have your dog out in the house when visitors come and he gets upset by them, put him away before you have visitors until he is happy to see them.

The best-case scenario would be to find a force-free trainer who uses these scientific principles of counter-conditioning. Never 'correct' a reaction, because you will create an association between 'bad things' happening and the trigger, and lose your progress.

NOTE: if you get a reaction, *you* made the mistake, not the dog. You're too close.

My Puppy is a Scaredy Cat
By Sally Bradbury

The world can be a scary place for a puppy sometimes, so it is important that we don't put him into situations that he cannot cope with.

If your puppy is scared of big, fat, bearded men in red coats, then you can just keep him away from the chimney on Christmas Eve. However, if your puppy is scared of everyday things, like the vacuum cleaner, the dog behind the fence up the road, or visitors to the house, then you will need to help him learn not to fear them.

Constant exposure to something that produces a fearful response will ensure that the puppy becomes increasingly fearful and there is the risk that it can become a real fear or phobia.

Let's take the vacuum cleaner as an example. There will be two stages to this, as vacuum cleaners *look* and *sound* scary. We can start by letting puppy see the 'scary monster' in the room and giving him a food treat every time he looks at it or investigates it. Once he is completely relaxed, we might push it or pull it a couple of inches across the carpet while puppy watches and enjoys a treat with each movement.

Before we plug in and turn on the vacuum cleaner, puppy needs to be as far away as possible, preferably in another room. You'll need a helper to turn on a stationary vacuum cleaner while you feed puppy a succession of treats. Over several sessions, he'll not only get used to the noise and sight of it moving, but he will associate it with the food and positive feelings instead of negative ones.

Counter-conditioning, which is pairing something positive with a low level of something scary, is not about changing behaviour, but about how the dog feels; it's about his emotional response.

Learn to recognise when your pup is scared. Allow him to retreat and watch from a distance. In the words of Debbie Jacobs of *Fearfuldogs.com*:

> 'I hate to sound flippant when people ask what they need to do to help their fearful dog and I say, stop scaring them. Don't do things to them that scare them. Don't put them into situations that scare them. Don't let other people or dogs scare them. Just stop scaring them.'

Trigger Stacking
By Abby Huxtable

Have you ever found your dog reacting in a situation they wouldn't usually react to? Or have they suddenly had a severe reaction to something they aren't usually bothered by? You have no idea why they have suddenly reacted like this when they wouldn't normally. Well, this reaction is likely due to trigger stacking.

My favourite analogy for this is a bucket. Your dog's bucket holds ten litres of water. Every event in your dog's life adds or takes water out of their bucket. However, if the bucket reaches that ten litres, it will overflow, and your dog will reach their threshold and react.

Each dog will have different values to things they experience. For example, food may be one litre, play may be one litre, the postal delivery or doorbell may be three litres, a cat could be two litres. A calming activity like scent work may be minus one litre, chewing may be minus one litre, a massage from your owner may be minus one litre.

The other key thing to remember is that cortisol is a stress hormone. This is produced in our dogs in exciting or stressful times and can take up to 72 hours to leave their bodies. That means you need to consider your bucket over a 72-hour (three day) period and even longer if you have a series of threshold events.

Let's look at this in a real-life scenario. Most dogs will hover around four or five litres in their buckets most of the time. This gives them a good capacity for additional stress events before they reach their threshold. Even if the dog were to wake up with their bucket completely empty, they then have their breakfast (+1L) and have a play with their owner (+1L = 2L in bucket). They then have a sniff in the garden (-1L = 1L in bucket). The owner takes the dog for a walk and they see a cat (+2L) then a tractor (+2L = 5L in bucket). This is still fine; they can cope with all of this. When they get home from the walk, they have an enrichment activity while owner is busy (-1L = 4L in bucket).

However, then a repair worker comes to the house (+3L = 7L in bucket), closely followed by a parcel delivery (+2L = 9L in bucket). We are now very close to threshold, but the dog still hasn't gone over their capacity. As the owner doesn't know about trigger stacking, they aren't aware that they might need to manage the dog's exposure to stress.

They head out on their afternoon walk and it is a nice sniffy walk (-1L = 8L in bucket), but then at the end of the walk they see another dog, who barks at them as they approach (+3L = 11L in bucket!!). Oh dear; our dog barks, lunges and is pulling on the end of the lead.

Our poor owner is shocked and mortified and says the common, 'I'm so sorry, he doesn't usually react like this'. However, both dogs were on leads so there's no real harm done. Both owners move on. Our owner wonders if it was something about the other dog that triggered them, as they are usually fine with other dogs, although a bit more wary if the other dog barks.

No! It was trigger stacking. Those events over this past day have overflowed our dog's bucket. This same scenario could have played out over the space of three days with the same result (although it's likely there would be more activities that empty the bucket).

Obviously, if you have a dog that is reactive to several triggers, they will have a much fuller bucket in general and reach their threshold much quicker. This is why we recommend at least three days off after a stress event to really ensure that bucket is fully empty before we expose our dogs to more stressors.

This is also why we work with our dogs to desensitise them and counter-condition them to triggers. So, instead of a trigger being worth four litres, it is maybe only one or two litres. You see this as you work through counter-conditioning. Your dog reacts less and recovers quicker from stress events as the litre value of the trigger reduces.

We also use plenty of calming activities, those licking, sniffing, and chewing activities, plus enrichment activities (as long as they are not frustrating or exciting for our dogs), to reduce the amount of water in our dogs' buckets. Of course, time itself will allow that cortisol to dissipate and the water to naturally evaporate from the bucket.

Therefore, if your dog has an unexpected reaction to something that doesn't usually bother them, think back over your last few days. What events have occurred that could have contributed to filling that bucket?

If you have a reactive dog, who you know has several triggers, give them plenty of time off between exposure to these triggers to allow that bucket to empty. This way, you prevent them from reaching threshold.

Plan your desensitisation and counter-conditioning sessions so there are calming activities in between, as well as time off. Don't risk pushing them over that threshold by exposing them to too many triggers in a short space of time.

Reactive Dogs
The importance of stress levels and working under threshold
By Jo Maisey

There is never any substitute for consulting a qualified and experienced behaviourist, who will be able to see what the cause of the problem is, give you advice on managing the problem, and then look at fixing the problem.

The following advice will do no harm and put you on the right road until you can see a behaviourist. In this instance, I am using the example of a dog who is reactive to other dogs, but the same principles can apply to other situations that a dog may react to.

What is a Reactive Dog?
A reactive dog is one that will bark, growl, lunge, snap, and so on at certain things (stimuli), such as dogs, people, or traffic. Living with a reactive dog can be incredibly stressful, not to mention embarrassing for the person on the other end of the lead.

Socialising
The time for socialising dogs, that is, getting them used to anything and everything so that they are comfortable with what life throws at them, is when they are puppies – up to around 16 weeks of age. After that, you're into a programme of counter-conditioning (turning around their underlying emotional response) and de-sensitising. Merely exposing

them to things they find scary is very unlikely to change their underlying emotional response and may make them more reactive.

Settling into a New Home

When any dog, no matter how well adjusted, goes to a new home, she is bound to find things a little scary. Everything is new. She doesn't know her way around. She doesn't know what is expected of her. She doesn't know the people in the new house or whether she can trust them. In the early days, I tend to keep things low key and her world quite small. That way, she can become used to things slowly and gently without having a whole load of things to deal with all at once.

Stress, and therefore adrenalin levels, need to be given a chance to come down. I would avoid anything that a dog finds scary/is reactive to initially, otherwise you might find yourself in an ever-increasing cycle of reactivity.

Initially, dogs are often worried about things, but not relaxed enough to show how they feel. After they have relaxed, they then feel able to tell you they are not comfortable about some situations – perhaps other dogs or certain people being near them.

Fear and Reactivity

Reactive dogs are usually fearful. Truly confident dogs do not need to give a big show; they can make the other dog go away by using some very subtle body language. Fear is reflexive, emotional, and not something a dog can help doing. By being reactive, they are making the other dog go away! While on lead, they do not have the choice of flight from the fight/flight response, so must resort to fight. This may become a learned behaviour – after all, it's a strategy that works!

Management and Dealing with the Problem

This is how I would approach it:

- Keep things low key to allow adrenalin/stress levels to drop. Stressed dogs cannot learn
- Set up to succeed. This means avoiding any areas where you think she may kick off. If you see another dog, turn around, walk the other way, cross the road, body block, hide behind a tree, put her behind your legs; whatever it takes to avoid the other dog. Don't put her in a position where she feels the need to defend herself. Apart from allowing her stress levels to drop, this will have the added benefit of her learning to trust you and that you will deal with the scary thing, so she has no need to

- Remember that any time there is an incident, her stress levels will rise, meaning that she is likely to be more reactive for the next few days. While her stress levels are raised, she may not be able to cope with things that she would ordinarily manage
- Trigger stacking – say the level at which she reacts is a ten. The postal delivery is a four, so she doesn't react. A kid on a bike is another four, totalling eight, but still below her threshold of ten, so she doesn't react. Then she sees a car. This is only a two and so there would normally be no reaction at all, but added to the previous eight, it's tipped her over threshold and so she will react. Trigger stacking explains why a usually non-reactive dog may react to seemingly non-scary things. Imagine this goes on day after day! An ever increasing spiral and the dog ends up reacting to everything!
- Once her adrenalin/stress levels have dropped, you can start to work on her underlying emotional response
- You need to work sub-threshold. This is **very important**. Stressed dogs cannot learn. The threshold is a distance at which she can see the scary thing, but **not react**. This is called the critical distance. Sometimes it can be a massive distance! It can also change from day to day and even hour to hour, depending on what's happened previously, and where her stress levels are at. It also depends on how scary the other dog is. Direct eye contact is challenging. A direct approach is challenging. Squashed faced dogs and docked dogs are more difficult to read. Dogs with an upright stance and pricked ears are challenging. So, the critical distance is not set in stone. It's better to be further away than you think you need to be, than too close and therefore elicit a reaction
- Now we need to look at changing the underlying emotional response. Currently her response to seeing another dog is, 'OH MY GOD!!! IT'S A SCARY THING!!! I NEED TO MAKE IT GO AWAY'. We want to change that to 'Oh look. Another dog. Goody! Where's my sausage!'
- The way to do that is to pair the scary thing with something she finds incredibly rewarding. The easiest thing is food. Very yummy food. Food that she never gets at any other time, so kibble won't cut it! Liver cake? Roast chicken? Whatever it takes. The size of the food needs to be tiny; about pea-sized and you need lots of it! It needs to be tiny as you don't want to have to wait while she chews it. There needs to be lots of it so that you can continually feed her one bit at a time

- So, once the scary thing (another dog) is in *her* sight (it's very important that she sees it and is sub-threshold), then you start shovelling the yummy food down her throat. It's very important that she **sees** the dog and **then** you start to feed her immediately. Once the dog is out of **her** sight, then you stop feeding her. That way, the dog becomes a *predictor* of yummy stuff. If you feed her before she sees the dog, then the food will become a predictor of scary things!
- You are not asking her for any particular behaviour or to do anything other than be aware of the dog at this point. Remember, fear is an emotional, reflexive response, and something she cannot help. You will not be reinforcing it by rewarding her, as emotions cannot be reinforced
- If she would normally take treats but won't, then the likelihood is that you are too close. Stressed dogs won't eat
- If she reacts, then you are probably too close and there is no point in trying to do anything. Best to just walk away and try again another day
- If you are not already, it would be best to walk her on a harness, perhaps with a double-ended/training lead clipped to both her harness and collar for safety. If she is reacting/lunging on just a collar, it is likely to cause her pain. She is then likely to associate the pain with the other dog and this will make her more reactive. Do not use a choke chain or slip lead, as these will cause pain. Dogs learn by association

Over time, you should see the critical distance reduce, and her looking to you for yummy stuff when she sees another dog. How long this will take is a bit of a piece of string question!

Summary
1. Allow stress levels to drop.
2. Apply management techniques to avoid triggers and set up for success. You don't want it to become a learned/ingrained behaviour, so you want to avoid her practising it.
3. Follow a programme of systematic desensitisation.

Real life happens. Don't get disheartened if things go a bit wrong and she reacts. Just try again another time. The mistake most of us make is trying to take things too quickly, not listening to our dogs nor taking it at their pace. We've all been there!

Reactive Dog Myths

By Zara Lipsett, Wagging Wonders Lincoln
http://www.waggingwonderslincoln.co.uk/

Dogs who bark and lunge at other dogs or people are often very worried dogs. It can be a big challenge to live with a reactive dog who is struggling with triggers and walks. There are a lot of myths out there, too, which don't help.

Myth: You Aren't Firm Enough with your Dog

I hear this one often. People contacting me with reactive dogs, under the impression that it is because they were 'too soft' with their dogs or not firm enough. The reality is that reactivity has very little to do with rules or firmness. Reactivity is generally an emotional response, which needs addressing to ensure the dog becomes more confident. Being 'firm' or harsh often has the opposite effect.

Myth: Your Rescue Must have been Abused

A lot of people assume their reactive rescue dog must have been abused if they are nervous and jumpy. However, this isn't strictly true. The dog's reactivity could have been a reason for surrender, or they might have had a bad experience with their trigger, or it could simply be poor genetics. Sometimes there is no obvious reason. It's important not to dwell on a rescue dog's past, instead focus on their future and how you can work together as a team.

Myth: Your Dog is Protecting You

Dogs are experts in self-preservation in the main. They tend to react to help themselves rather than to help you. While it is true that certain breeds might display guarding instincts or protection in the right circumstances, if a dog is regularly reacting to triggers, it is unlikely to be about you. Your dog is more concerned about themselves.

Myth: Your Dog needs Socialisation

Reactive dogs who are anxious or learning appropriate manners do *not* need to be 'socialised' around their triggers in a traditional sense. The critical socialisation period ends when a dog is still a puppy. Beyond that, a dog who develops reactivity issues needs careful and considerate exposure to boost positive experiences. Often, the worst thing you can do is take them on 'pack walks' or off lead sessions. These will likely just flood your dog and make the issue worse.

Fact: Your Reactive Dog is Having a Hard Time

A reactive dog is one who needs a careful plan of action to help them learn that they don't need to react to triggers and they do not need to worry so much. They need patience and understanding. Short cuts will interrupt progress. A modern dog trainer or behaviourist will be able to help you learn to read your dog, make plans to succeed and help you in your progress to help both you and your dog become more confident.

Noise Phobias and Fireworks

By Rebecca Köhnke

If your dog suffers from a noise phobia, it's important to have him checked by a vet before attempting any other measures. Recent research has shown that the presence of noise sensitivities in dogs is strongly linked to the presence of physical pain. When we find and treat the pain, the noise sensitivity often reduces.

We still need to help the dog with the actual fear, especially as there will be those dogs that experience fear due to a traumatic event, or something similar, and which is unrelated to pain.

Now the trouble with noise phobias is:

- The noises they fear are often pretty much out of our control and appear at random and varying times and volumes
- Dogs are so perfect at making connections. Fireworks happen in the dark. So therefore, anything after sundown is hell and a no-go. Where I live, fireworks happen during the days leading up to New Year. Most Christmas trees go up around Christmas Eve. Most firework phobic dogs freak at the sight of the Christmas tree. You get the idea
- Our dogs are also hugely efficient at generalising phobias. Fireworks started it. So, it's fireworks for a while. Then a bird scarer goes off. Wham – that was a bang, too. It reminds them of that awful night. Here comes the panic; then a gun, a door slamming, a branch breaking, rain on the conservatory, tin foil crinkling. This includes locations, too. That house over there, that's where the fireworks went off. That block around the corner, heard a balloon pop there once. It's the fear of fear itself that ultimately perpetuates these associations.

And unfortunately, without our intervention, **all** noise phobias will become worse over time.

So, we have our work cut out. We need to:

- First and foremost, keep the dog feeling safe
- Help them break all those seemingly random associations, and
- Counter-condition and desensitise to the scary noises

Now, here comes the real kicker. While working on these phobias, the dog must never be triggered to experience fear. We always need to keep them under threshold.

When a dog is 'only' phobic to certain noises, the phobia is usually manageable to a good degree.

We can:

- Avoid times and areas where the noises appear
- Build dens in the house and dull external noises as much as possible
- Teach the dog to wear mutt muffs
- Put fabric blinds on the conservatory roof to pull if rain is forecast (they're nice to keep the temperature down, too)
- Investigate the use of situational medications for those situations we can't avoid, like forecasted thunderstorms

More management ideas, as well as information on how to progress with desensitisation, can be found in this chapter.

Now, some dogs develop a general sound phobia; they're scared of pretty much all external noise. As you often have no control over environmental noises, this is very difficult. You really need to contact a behaviour savvy vet or vet behaviourist (VB) and get your dog on daily medication to help with the anxiety. This will give you a foot in the door. Without this, I promise, you will not be able to tackle the phobia, and it will get worse. There is very good medication available, but you willl need the help of someone with experience. Medication can stop the phobia from worsening if there is a slip-up or accidental exposure to noise, and so they are worth considering.

While you're working with your savvy vet/VB, you can help your dog by managing to avoid noises as much as possible:

- Get her used to wearing mutt muffs
- Find out times for all those repeatedly occurring noises. You can contact local offices/farmers to find out when shoots will be held, pigeons scared, trees felled, planes landed

- See if she will toilet just outside your fence or in your garden. Maybe inside a garden shelter. This might be the one occasion where I might advocate for puppy pads too

For all dogs fearful of anything, really, the following applies:

- Do not force/drag/carry a fearful dog outdoors. This is important!
- Please do continue to take her out if your dog enjoys it. It might be worth checking out places beforehand, so you can avoid those scary situations
- Please do comfort your dog. She already knows she's scared. Fear is not rational, it's an emotion. It's there, and true, and real for her, and she doesn't care if you confirm it or not. What she does care about though, is that she has a safe haven with you. Don't freak with her. But if comfort is what she asks for to help her calm down again, then please do so!
- Remember, she's at the mental level of an infant/very young toddler
- There are several sound desensitisation programmes available. **Start at the lowest volume!!!!** Your starting volume is one less than what causes your dog to twitch an ear. **Only increase volume when you get no more reaction!**
- Start in February for November fireworks season. You need a good six to nine months to work on this!
- Refresh in between fireworks seasons

These programmes are great for some dogs. For some, they lack the 'real fireworks' feeling, but they're a good starting point. They can be very helpful for preventing phobias in puppies too. Good speakers and/or Dolby surround helps.

Fireworks Season and Dogs
By Jo Maisey

Ideally, you would already have desensitised and counter-conditioned your dog to fireworks, but if you've not had time to do so, then you can try to mitigate the effects as much as possible. Sound phobias tend to *increase* if not addressed and generalise to the time of day or geographical area where the dog got scared.

My own dog was on Xanax (Alprazolam) as a situational med. However, I desensitised him to fireworks/thunder over the years and so he rarely had to take it. Even so, prescribed medications (after consultation with your vet) are far better than a freaked-out dog. There is also a relatively new med available from the vet called Sileo – an oral mucosal gel. I've heard good things about it.

These are my tips for keeping your dog safe and happy:

- Ensure your dog has been walked and toileted well before dark.
- Do not take your dog out after dark; not even into the garden. If your dog happens to be in the garden when a firework goes off, then they will associate the garden with scary things and be anxious about going into the garden (especially after dark) for some time to come
- Give your dog a safe den to go into and bunker down. A crate is a good place as long as your dog is already comfortable in one. Keep the crate away from external walls to negate the vibrations from big fireworks as much as possible. For the same reason, deep comfy bedding under and around the crate is a good idea. It soaks up the percussion. Quilts/duvets can be good for this
- Give your dog something excellent to chew/lick/gnaw while in their den and the fireworks are going off. Perhaps a raw, meaty bone, an antler, bull bar or similar. I give a frozen Kong. I fill the Kongs with a little kibble at the bottom (to stop everything running out), then pour in some natural yoghurt, mixed with a tin of tuna in spring water and some chopped up treats, such as sausage, chicken, or ham. Then I poke something like gravy bones in the top. Chewing and licking can be pacifying for a dog
- Ensure all doors, windows and curtains are closed before dark, so that your dogs can't see the flashes from the fireworks
- Turn on all TVs and radios to muffle the sound from the fireworks as much as possible
- If you have already discussed and been prescribed medication from your vet, use it. Ensure it is NOT ACP (acepromazine)
- If your dog has been helped by pheromones, such as Adaptil or Pet Remedy products, or pressure wraps, such as Thundershirts, then apply them before dark. The same goes for any supplements that you know will help your dog
- Just because a product is labelled 'natural', 'herbal', or something similar does not necessarily mean that it is 'safe'. Discuss with your vet before combining supplements as well as prescribed medication in case of contra-indications

- You may need to stay up late, until after the fireworks have finished, if you want your dog to toilet before bedtime. Be aware that your dog may be too worried to go out, even after the fireworks have long finished. It is better to spend a small amount of time clearing up an indoor accident than to risk a firework going off while your dog is outdoors

Fear of Car or Travel

By Jo Maisey

I tend to use free shaping to get a dog to jump in the car/van. It looks something like this, and I teach it in perhaps five-minute sessions over several days – maybe even weeks, depending on the dog:

- Have a clicker and a large amount of tiny, yummy treats in a bag/pot. You could also use her meal allowance if she finds her kibble high enough value; or maybe a mix of kibble and yummy treats. A marker word, such as 'Yes!' or 'Good!', can be used in place of a clicker, but a clicker has a unique sound
- Dog on a long lead
- Have the car/van door/boot open
- Take dog on lead only as far towards the car as she is happy to go and stop. Watch her body language closely to see at what point she no longer wants to approach the car
- Wait for dog to look at car. Click and treat (c/t)
- Repeat until dog is sure that it's the looking at the car that gets the c/t
- Up the criteria so that one step towards the car gets a c/t
- Back off again after the one step to reset
- At some point, she should start to offer two steps towards the car, but at all stages, it should be her choice. You just wait it out until she offers the behaviour. No luring. No forcing
- Continue in this manner until you end up next to the car. At each stage, she may offer more steps towards the car and you will need to retreat less of a distance to reset, so you end up next to the car
- Once at the car, you want her to offer some interaction with the car. Perhaps putting her head in to start with – c/t. Then one paw – c/t. Then two paws – c/t
- At some point she will jump in the car – c/t immediately and call her back out again
- Big game of jumping in the car, c/t and back out again
- Incrementally increase the length of time she is in the car by one second at a time before c/t and back out again

- Once happy with that, let her jump in the car and gradually begin to shut the door in increments before c/t and back out
- If she is happy to sit in the car, then leave her in there rather than getting her to jump out again. If you can get someone to help you, sit in the boot with her, get them to shut the door, c/t and they open it again
- Incrementally increase the time the door is shut before c/t and open
- So, at some point, you have a dog who is happy to jump in the boot and have the door closed
- Now, progress to getting in the boot, shut the door and have someone start the engine – c/t and turn the engine off
- Incrementally build up the time the engine is running
- Next stage is jump in, shut door, start engine, and move 10 feet – c/t and stop
- Incrementally increase the distance travelled

At every stage, the dog must be happy before moving on to the next stage. Happy means 'Wahay! What a fabulous game!'

This seems a long-winded process, but at all times you are ensuring she is never worried and it is her choice. You are setting her up to succeed.

Afraid of Visitors

By Sally Bradbury and Kay Bradnum

The first thing to consider is, does your dog need to meet these visitors? He certainly doesn't need to meet the gas engineer, repair people or delivery people. So, make sure that before you open the door, he's shut away safely in another room with something to occupy him. While he's in there, you can give him a few chew toys that are particularly interesting, because he only gets them on these occasions.

Then you can work on visitors who it would be helpful to have him comfortable with. If you have some stooge visitors that you can practise with, that will be useful.

Give him space; maybe put him in the kitchen with a baby gate across the doorway. Then when visitors come, you can feed him little treats to help him feel better about them. To give you time to greet the visitors, scatter several treats on the floor for him to search out. This is a calming activity. Once he seems more relaxed and they are sitting down (so are less threatening), you can let him out of the kitchen. Ask your visitors to ignore him completely (especially avoid eye contact) and wait for him to come to them. If he does come towards them, they could throw a treat behind him, so he gets a double reward: the treat and the relief of moving away again. Don't ask the visitors to give treats as he will be lured close to eat it, then panic once he's eaten the food and realises he's too close. If visitors ignore him other than to throw treats past him, it will hopefully not be long before he's approaching them for attention. If not, that's no big deal; he should be able to choose to be left in peace if that's what he needs.

Make sure he has a safe place to go to. It can be a bed tucked out of the way somewhere or a crate, if he loves his crate. Always have it available for him to retreat to whenever he feels the need.

Your aim should be for a dog who is comfortable and relaxed when visitors arrive. He may never want a fuss from people outside his immediate family and that's OK. He's not their dog after all!

Chapter 5

Recall

Teaching Recall
By Sally Bradbury

Recall is less about coming when called and more about having a dog that wants to be with you.

There are lots of things you can do. Hand feeding, clicker training, playing tug or fetch, teaching collar touches and hand targeting, encouraging the dog to check in and reinforcing any desirable behaviours heavily can all contribute to building a solid recall.

Most important, though, is to prevent the behaviour you do not want, especially something that is very self-rewarding. such as running off to play with another dog.

Long Line

Have your dog on a long line attached to a harness. In a safe, fenced area the line can trail. When you want her back, you either wait for her to finish running or you stand on the line when the opportunity arises and walk along it to her.

In an area where you need to keep hold of the line, you will need to keep it relatively short. Let it out longer when appropriate and shorten it again if necessary. This is an art form, which you should practise in a safe area so that if you are worried she will pull you over, you can just let go.

Hand Feeding

Feeding her from your hand outdoors is an effective way of getting focus on you. Start in the garden. Every mealtime, put her food in your pocket or a food pouch, go to the garden, and feed a handful at a time when she is in front of you, wanting the food. Step back, say her name excitedly, feed. Repeat. She doesn't have to do anything except step towards you and want to eat.

Two or three weeks of this and you should be able to go to the field or park and do this at mealtimes. No running about if she has a full tummy, just go there to eat, and come home again. Then when you are there for exercise, treats can be used to reinforce her for being there with you.

Clicker Training

If she is clicker trained, then you can click and treat any behaviour that you like. For recall, I would click & treat just a glance back at you or looking at you as she walks past. You can throw her the treat and not even need her to come right back to you for the first stages. Gradually, you would shape the behaviour into the complete recall. You add the cue once she's doing it reliably and, of course, she usually gets dismissed to go again.

Playing

Toys can be devalued if she has them all the time. Let her have a chew toy or two and keep the favourites for playing with together. Tug of war is a great bonding game. For the most part, play outdoors rather than indoors, because this can make a lot of difference to the attention your dog gives you when out.

Collar Touch

Teaching a collar touch just means that every time you want to give her a treat, a fuss, her dinner, let her in the garden, or anything else of value, you take hold of her collar prior to giving her the thing she wants. This is actually a very powerful exercise, and the result is that the dog will eventually move her neck towards your hand any time she wants one of the rewards.

Hand Target

Teaching a hand target is similar. It's easy to clicker train a dog to touch your hand with their nose and can be paired with the collar touch for maximum effect.

Check In

Teaching a check in and reinforcing desirable behaviours starts indoors. Set yourself a challenge. Put twenty treats aside in a pot in the kitchen and every time she looks at you (not when you ask her to), give her a treat. Count the treats left at the end of the day. Next day, try and beat your record. Then take it to the garden. Lower your expectations for this. And then, eventually, out and about.

Premack

One of the biggest reasons for a dog not recalling is because there is something better on offer if they don't come back. Premack is all about using the rewards the dog wants. Play with the dog, chase the squirrel, or pee on the tree – what the dog wants, the dog can have (if appropriate) for checking in with you first or coming when called. It's a good solution for the problem of what to do when she sees another dog.

Enlist the help of some willing friends with dogs. Arrange to meet someone with a dog, who will appear at a strategic point. Have your dog on her long trailing line. When she sees the dog, stand on her line and the other dog will stop approaching as pre-arranged. Call her back to you. She can choose to stay where she is and look at the dog in the distance or come back to you and be released to go and play. It will take a few repetitions for her to learn how to earn the reward that she wants. You will need several sessions with several different dogs, and you will also need to vary the rewards. She doesn't always get to go and play because it won't always be appropriate; sometimes she gets food, sometimes a game with you.

Your aim is for her to eventually see a dog and return to you when off lead. This gives you time to ascertain whether it would be appropriate to allow her to go and see the dog.

Be Fun to Be With

Once you have added value to your attention, toys, and treats, I'd suggest that when you get to the field/park, you start tossing treats for your puppy to catch, get a tug toy from your pocket and have a game for ten to twenty seconds, then run about and have her chase you. Do some collar touches, hand targets, whatever else she likes to do with you, all still on lead and with the line attached (to a harness), as well. More treats, more play, drop the lead, pick up the lead, unclip the lead, put the lead back on – all while feeding and playing. Do this for a minute or two and finish with lead off, putting toy and treats back in your pocket, and tell her, 'Off you go'.

Whichever way she goes, you go the other way. Give her some sniff time, then start cheering and whooping and running again, get the toy and treats out again, and repeat ad infinitum.

The one thing you shouldn't do when letting your dog off lead is ask her to sit and wait and then take the lead off and let her go. She'll spend that waiting time scanning the horizon and anticipating the release.

When you get to the field or park with your dog, you want her thinking, 'Is she going to feed me, is she going to play with me, or is she going to tell me to go?' When you let her off the lead, you want her thinking, 'Is she going to feed me, is she going to play with me, or is she going to tell me to go?'

Choosing and Using a Long line

By Claire Martin

When to Use One?

Long lines are useful training tools that enable owners to give their dogs a bit of freedom, safe in the knowledge that they can't get into trouble, run away, or get lost. They are also useful training tools to teach a reliable recall. They are great for young puppies and dogs going through adolescence, and are essential for newly adopted rescue dogs.

How Long?

Long lines typically come in either 5 or 10 metre lengths, but some manufacturers make them longer or shorter.

What Type?

Cheap webbing long lines can be bought from pet shops, but they will absorb water, mud, and indeed anything that the line drags through on the ground, which can include manure and grit. Considering that you will need to handle these lines all the time, this is a disadvantage.

Horse lunge lines come in bright colours, but they are often quite heavy for smaller dogs and have a heavy trigger clip. They also absorb water and grit when they trail on the ground.

Biothane is rubberised webbing that doesn't get wet or absorb grit. It comes in many widths and colours and can be cut to any length. In narrower widths, it's ideal for puppies and small dogs. In the wider widths, it's strong enough for the largest dogs. It is also much less likely to cause a friction burn when you use it due to the nature of the material, which isn't rough on your hands.

Yellow Dog

The use of yellow accessories can indicate that a dog is reactive, so a yellow long line is a great idea.

How to Use Them?

A long line should always be attached to a dog's harness and never to their collar. If a dog does run to the end of the line, stopping the dog in its harness will not put pressure on the dog's neck. Ideally, you would teach your dog a 'steady' cue, so they know that they are coming to the end of the line.

Checking In

Start off using the long line by looping it all into one hand. Let the line out as the dog moves away from you and loop it back in as they come nearer to you. That way there is no tangle risk. Every time your dog chooses to come back, reward them with a high-value treat, then let them go off wandering again.

Don't be tempted to keep calling them. Just let them sniff and wander until they come back on their own. We are trying to teach them a voluntary check in here rather than a recall. Keep walking and keep the line loose between you and the dog.

If you reward every time they come back, you will soon find that they keep coming back for a reward. Once you are sure that they will repeatedly check in, let the line drag on the ground and just walk.

Reward every time your dog comes back. If your dog starts to wander too far, stand on the line, gather it back up and go back to the first step. Only take the long line off if you are sure that your dog will keep checking in with you.

Don't ever feel it's a failure to put the long line back on and always use a long line in an unfamiliar environment.

Recall

When you are fairly certain that your dog was just about to come back to you to check in, call your dog and reward like crazy! This should only be after your dog is checking in regularly on a long line, and before you decide to drop the line. Do this at random. Reward this behaviour more than checking in because this time you asked your dog to come rather than them coming back of their own accord. You shouldn't consider dropping the long line to drag behind your dog until you have a very reliable recall.

Why not a Flexi Lead?

A flexi lead keeps tension on the line attached to your dog. This means that they aren't making their own choice to come back and they get used to pulling; something we don't want to happen. The mechanism inside the handle can break and, sadly, dogs have been hurt or killed when the brake hasn't stopped them running out in front of a car. Lastly, and most seriously, if the handle of the flexi is dropped (and it's hard not to drop it if the brake mechanism fails) and your dog is at top speed when the line becomes fully extended, then the handle will travel behind the dog, scaring it and making it run ever faster until it comes to harm or collapses. Cord flexi leads can also cause horrid burns if you try to grab the line to stop your dog. We don't recommend them!

Prey Drive

By Sally Bradbury

I have a dog who is very prey driven.

Here are some of the things I did with him, and still do on occasions.

For about a three-month period after I first took him on, or at least when I discovered we had a problem, he ate all his food outdoors from my hand. He didn't have to do anything for it except take it and eat it as I said his name excitedly and stepped back a pace or two.

We started in the garden. After a while, we went out for dinner and often went to the woods, his favourite hunting ground. He was on a long line and harness of course.

At first, I would just feed him his dinner there, but eventually I only offered him a handful of dinner when his ears pricked and he saw, smelled, or heard something. This then became the trigger to turn to me and eat. Hear a rustle, eat.

The other thing I would do was to go hunting with him, again with the long line on his harness. I would just follow on behind him and encourage him to find scents and follow them. Of course, I would never encourage him or allow him to actually frighten or harm another animal. It was just pretend hunting, but he didn't know that.

He is also a bird chaser, so I enlisted the help of the crows. I had already taught him an awesome distant down and so, when appropriate, I would give him the OK to chase the bird as a reward for lying down. If it was not appropriate, he would return to me for a different reward, or I would collect him from his down stay.

Then there is an exercise called the predictive cue. His was 'toy'. Every single time I threw a toy he heard the word 'toy'. So, if I then threw a toy and didn't say the word, but immediately threw another toy in a different direction and did use the word, he was immediately distracted from chasing the first thing he saw moving and went for the second simply because of the power of the word 'toy'.

Does he still chase things? Occasionally, but if I am paying attention, I can recall him straight away.

Read about Billy in the early days here:
http://badboybillysblog.blogspot.com/

Chapter 6

Resource Guarding

Resource Guarding: Normal or Not?

By Emma Judson

Resource guarding has become a rather common term discussed by both trainers and pet owners. However, along the way, the meaning has become a little blurred and I feel this is not helping owners determine how serious a problem is, or whether they need help to address it.

So what's normal and what isn't? What can we address ourselves and what might indicate that we need to seek professional help?

Normal:

- Hungry dog gobbling down food quicker as someone approaches
- Hungry dog freezing and staring while eating a bone as someone approaches
- Not particularly hungry dog with a vast bone he can't eat all at once, freezing and staring or picking up the bone and moving away as someone approaches
- Dog actively eating a bone growls and/or snaps if startled by someone trying to remove the bone
- Dog actively eating from a bowl growls and/or snaps if startled by someone trying to take the bowl
- Playful dog picks up toy and moves it away from another dog or person approaching to take it
- Dog puts paw across toy while lying down when another dog or person approaches to take it

These are all examples at the normal end of the scale. While you could argue that a toy is not a valuable resource necessary for the survival of the dog, I don't think it is abnormal for pet dogs to view toys as valuable resources, even if a wild canid would not.

Abnormal:

- Not at all hungry dog growls when someone tries to pick up a dropped piece of kibble ten feet from the dog
- Dog flies across the room to bite someone picking up an empty dog bowl
- Dog bites someone without any prior warning for picking up an empty mug near the dog
- Dog growls and air snaps when sat with a person and someone else or another dog approaches
- Dog appears to be guarding a space or something invisible and growls or snaps if a person approaches

These are not normal reactions. In these examples, we have dogs going to extreme lengths that create risk for them, over items that are not theirs and have very little value or no value at all. Some of these incidences may not be about guarding an item at all, but about the dog protecting themselves. It is likely that all these dogs are experiencing other problems, possibly pain. Some of them may have been taught by humans that the polite stages of freeze, lip curl, growl, air snap, and so on, simply do not work. They have therefore been pushed by humans into going straight for the bite.

All of these situations would warrant an owner getting professional help, because it is likely there's far more going on than simply protecting a resource. Some prior training may possibly have added to the problem.

To determine whether a resource guarding dog is dangerous, we need to look at several factors:

- How predictable is the dog's behaviour?
- Does the dog stay with the item they are guarding? Or do they come away from it? That is, are they defensive or offensive?
- How big is the dog?
- What is the dog guarding?

The combinations of these factors tell us just how dangerous the issue actually is.

So, let's consider a small breed puppy who holds his juicy bone in his teeth and growls when his owner is six feet away. He doesn't move from where he is, or only moves away from his person. He only performs this behaviour when he has a juicy bone, and lives with two adults who only have adult visitors.

While this situation almost certainly worries the owner, it isn't particularly dangerous. It is predictable. It is defensive rather than offensive. The dog is small. The dog is guarding something very high in value that he only gets because it is given to him and we therefore know exactly when this is going to happen.

What about the giant breed who guards scraps of tissue, which the owner's small children often leave lying around? He guards offensively and moves away from the tissue, towards a person. This can happen in any room, and his owners have punished him by shouting at him and smacking him for stealing tissues in the past. He has bitten in this situation several times.

109

This one is obviously dangerous. He is a big dog and there are children in the house, who are at greater risk from a large dog than adults would be. His access to the item that he guards is unpredictable and cannot easily be controlled. The scraps of tissue are also also small enough that he could have one without anyone realising until he reacts. He comes away from the item to bite, and he has previously associated warning language, such as growling, freezing, staring, lip curling, and so on, with punishment, so he no longer gives any warning.

Both scenarios are important to take note of, but the first dog is behaving normally and this situation can easily be addressed. By pairing the presence of people (at a distance the dog is comfortable with) with tasty, high-value treats when the dog has a bone, we can change the dog's emotional response from 'argh, stay away' to 'ooh goody, more yummies'..

We can also simply not give him a bone should there be children visiting or anyone who is likely to ignore the instructions to leave him alone.

It would be easy to turn this puppy into a dog with a serious problem, however, by following dangerous advice to punish his growling and take his bone from him forcibly each time he does it. So, it's really important to be aware of what's going on and why, and to take the appropriate action.

The second dog is dangerous and the whole family is at risk. To address this dog's problem, they would need to remove all access to tissues, stop using aversives and punishment, and try to retrain their dog to growl to warn them of how he feels. That's not an easy task and one that won't be achieved until the owners understand why punishment is not a suitable method to alter behaviour. It is unlikely that the owners could achieve a safe environment to alter the dog's behaviour, anyway, due to having vulnerable household members. In this case, there are children in the family, but the elderly or infirm may also be at risk. I would want a professional to see this dog and would likely recommend rehoming to a safer environment. If that were not possible, then euthanasia should be seriously considered. While no-one wants to hear that, in some cases, it is the only responsible option.

The following articles discuss some of the more common resource guarding situations and how to deal with them appropriately. If at any point you are not sure of what to do, the best advice is to keep everyone safe and seek professional help.

Prevention of Resource Guarding
By Sally Bradbury

Although this is written about puppies, it applies equally to adult dogs.

Preventing food guarding at mealtimes is easy. Allow puppy to eat in peace. If you have more than one dog, then feed them separately and teach them that humans near their food bowl are always there for the sole purpose of adding a tasty treat to the bowl.

Don't be persuaded that you need to take your dog's food away or put your hand in the bowl while they eat to make them tolerant, because you risk doing exactly the opposite and triggering resource guarding.

What is slightly more difficult when you have a puppy is preventing the guarding of found or 'stolen' items. Puppies tend to investigate every object they find by picking it up in their mouths. It could be stones from the garden, the children's toys, or anything else that you left within reach. This is particularly relevant to gun dog breeds because they are hardwired to pick up and carry, and always want to have something in their mouth.

By forcibly taking items from your pup's mouth, especially if you also get a little cross with them for picking it up, you are running the risk of teaching the puppy to avoid you and, when caught, to guard the possession that is now theirs and you are trying to steal.

The solution is to teach your puppy to 'give' so that you never have to 'take'.

To do this, sit on the floor with a pile of toys and encourage puppy to bring them back after you have rolled them away. By sitting on the floor, you are not tempted to move towards him. When he comes close while he is holding something, then tell him what a good boy he is while giving him bum or shoulder scritches. Do not put your hand near his mouth. Do not want what he has in his mouth.

He will probably drop the toy at some point and then you can throw it again. If he's a foodie, then a food reward for dropping is a good plan. Don't use food as a bribe, though. Only fetch it from your pocket after he drops the toy. Once he's happily bringing toys and dropping them in your lap or your hand, add in other items; coasters, tea towels, anything that he might like to 'steal'. Then start working on him fetching stationary items as opposed to something you throw. Then generalise it to anywhere in the house. Leave things for him to pick up so that you can praise and reward him for doing so.

111

If you approach this the right way, you should end up with a dog that will bring you anything he finds, regardless of whether he should have it or not. He will still be satisfying his need to find, hold and carry, but won't be 'stealing' things he shouldn't have. You may consider it a chore to have your dog bringing things to you all the time, but it's preferable to stealing and guarding, and it can be toned down later by only rewarding if you ask him to 'fetch'.

If your puppy is already guarding 'stolen' items, then it is important that you don't leave anything dangerous or valuable within his reach while you teach him an alternative behaviour. If he does get hold of something, then either let him have it or, if it's unsafe, create a diversion; you could knock on the door, scatter food on the floor, or get his lead out for a walk. This will only work once or twice, so keep it for an emergency.

If your puppy is already guarding food, resting places, toys, or even you, then please seek professional advice from a reputable, force-free trainer or behaviourist.

Food Aggression and Jess
My lovely food-aggressive girl
By Kay Bradnum

Jess is a medium-sized lurcher, who came to me when she was 15 months old. She had been living with a young girl, who loved her very much but could no longer care for her. Her owner had done the best she could, but I believe she was given some very poor advice. Jess had had very little socialisation and, from her behaviour when she came to us, I am very sure her owner was told to take the food bowl from her occasionally 'to make sure you can if you need to'. This is a sure-fire way to teach a dog that it needs to guard.

By the time Jess came to live with me, she was convinced she could lose her food at any time. When I put her food down, all she would do was pace up and down in front of it, snatching the odd mouthful, and growling constantly. She would snatch any food she could reach and warn all dogs very clearly that they would be in a world of pain if they came near her!

It was obvious that Jess was very stressed and struggling to cope with life.

Meals

The first thing I did was to put her food bowl in a separate room (utility room). Each mealtime, she was fed in there with the door shut. In time, Jess realised that no one was going to take her food and she began to relax. After about a month, I started leaving the door open so she could hear and see us, but I still made sure no one went in the utility room until Jess had left of her own accord. I have four dogs, so the others were all fed separately, and all bowls were picked up and washed immediately. This is good practise in any case for anyone with several dogs. Some dogs are fine fed together, but I don't take the chance.

Once was I sure Jess was tucking in and eating her food happily and confidently, I would walk in and quickly out of the room again. At first, her body would tense and she would freeze, but she soon understood that this was not a threat. Then I would walk through the utility room, past her (while she was eating), to the back door, and back again. Once she was happy with this, I started dropping a bit of sausage or cheese in the bowl as I went past. It took a while, but I knew I had won when Jess started to look around for her treat whenever I went in the room. I built up to the point that, when I put the sausage in her bowl and my hand was right next to her head, she wouldn't even bat an eyelid.

I know some people like to pick the bowl up, add the treat, and put it back down. I don't think that's necessary. I like to be left to eat in peace, and I think my dogs have the same right. I don't give them a bowl of food unless they can have it. Why would I need to take it away again?

Treats

Larger treats were only ever given in a separate room, and Jess was kept separate from the others until she had finished. This is no longer necessary, but all dogs are supervised, and I spread the dogs out before treating.

Smaller treats which could be eaten immediately weren't too much of a problem. Jess got hers first, and then the others in order, so everyone knew which treat was theirs. I also use each dog's name before dishing out bits of sausage or cheese, so they know which is theirs.

Scraps on the Floor

I had a couple of scares, where Jess would attack any dog closer to a crumb on the floor than she was. She has taught me to be very tidy in the kitchen (she's a dreadful thief anyway so counters are always kept clear) and my kitchen floor is regularly swept. I have relaxed this a little now, but I'm still careful if meat is involved, especially chicken, which is her favourite.

Teaching Jess to Give up her 'Treasures'
While all this was going on, I taught Jess a good, solid 'swap'. I started with stuff she didn't really want, something like a toy she had lost interest in, a bit of paper, or anything else that had little value to her. Then I said `swap', took it back, and gave her something she would like, such as a bit of sausage or cheese, or a quick game of tug. She's a bright girl and soon caught on. Nowadays, if she has something I'd rather she didn't, I can say 'Hey Jess! Swap?' and she immediately spits out whatever she has because she knows something better is coming.

This would work equally well for any dog who likes to steal objects. To start with, leave them with an object that doesn't matter. If it is readily available, *and* the dog doesn't get any attention from you, then it will lose value. You can also start working on a 'swap'.

Emergencies
I have been lucky. Jess has never had anything I needed from her urgently, but I've no doubt such a situation could arise. If this had occurred before I had taught 'swap', I could have run into the garden excitedly, or rang the doorbell, or offered a walk. Anything to grab her attention and distract her in a hurry. Of course, if you do this you have to give them a game in the garden or take them for a walk; otherwise, they will soon get wise. In the real world, there are very few emergencies that absolutely must be dealt with. I may have had to sacrifice the odd bacon butty, though I have learned to store food in the microwave if I must turn my back!

Chicken
I would say Jess is still a risk to other dogs when chicken is around. She seems to have a real addiction to it, so if we are eating it, she is separated while I'm cooking. We eat at the table alone, and all bones and leftovers are binned or fridged before the dogs are allowed in again. I could perhaps work hard on changing her behaviour around chicken, but our regime works just fine for us. Sometimes management is the best solution, and asking her to show restraint around chicken would be like asking an alcoholic to show restraint around whisky… Or me to show restraint around chocolate!

I have accepted this as one of her quirks, and I don't think a dog always has to be perfectly behaved to be a perfect dog!

Resource Guarding Owner

By Sally Bradbury

One of my dogs started to resource guard me when he was younger and would growl and grumble if the other dogs approached when we were interacting.

Instinct tells you to walk away and leave him so that he has nothing to guard, but all that does is confirm that he was right. The approach of another dog means I lose Mum.

So, I counter-conditioned him by giving him high-value treats when other dogs approached until he was practically inviting them over.

I started with Moss in a crate and would call a dog over, making sure to leave enough distance between the two that Moss would not react. I fed them both treats, but with Moss getting the lion's share. Before long we could do it without a crate.

I also had the issue of him grumbling when he was on the bed and another dog wanted to come up, so I used ear massages as his 'good thing' to associate with the approach of another dog.

Chapter 7

Loose Lead Walking (LLW)

General Advice before you Start
by Sally Bradbury

Remember to keep your training sessions very short and fun. Several two-minute training sessions throughout the day will be much more beneficial than one long one. Not having an on lead walk will be better than one where your dog pulls some of the time. So, if you can, drive to somewhere where your dog can have a good run around until he has learnt his new walking skills.

Start the training in the house, then the back garden, then the front garden, then the front garden with the gate open, then through the gate and back again, then to the lamppost and back. Only move on when the previous stage is nailed. Go back a stage if the training regresses.

Every time you attach his lead, it must be training.

We recommend a harness with a Y-shaped front and two points of attachment, chest and back, with a double-ended lead. This will turn your dog comfortably if he does pull, without causing any pain or damage to the neck.

Examples of such harnesses are:

- Perfect Fit
- Ruffwear Front Range
- TTouch
- Mekuti
- Dog Copenhagen

Loose Lead Walking
By Jo Maisey

Why do Dogs Pull on the Lead?

Dogs enjoy running about and exploring the outside world, usually at a faster pace than we walk. Dogs pull on the lead because we are slow and boring and pulling seems to get them where they want to go, which is usually somewhere more exciting!

When you allow your dog to pull, she learns that pulling gets her where she wants to go, so pulling is rewarded! It often becomes an ingrained habit.

Physically holding a dog back seems to invoke an oppositional, reflexive, pull response. Therefore, the harder you pull on the lead, the more your dog will pull against you and she may well get frustrated.

Why Should I Teach my Dog to Walk on a Loose Lead?

A dog who has been taught to walk on a lead without pulling is a delight to walk. People are much happier to walk a dog who has been well trained and as a result, the dog often gets more walks and goes to more places with their owners.

Teaching a dog to walk on a loose lead can help teach your dog to give you attention, and control her impulses in the presence of other dogs or other animals that she may like to chase.

A dog that has been taught to respond well to the lead can easily be removed from any potentially stressful situations.

Pulling on a lead can bring about physical problems for a dog. They have an unbalanced and strained posture, which can lead to back, neck, trachea, eye, and nerve issues, among others.

A dog that pulls on the lead can be a cause of frustration and embarrassment for the person on the other end of the lead. Sometimes this can lead to a situation where an owner is unable to walk their dog at all, which means that the dog does not get enough exercise or stimulation. This can give rise to an ever-increasing cycle of frustration for both the owner and the dog, plus the dog is likely to develop behavioural problems connected with lack of exercise and stimulation.

How do I Achieve Loose Lead Walking?

The lead is an important management and training tool and keeps your dog safe. It should always be loose, unless you need to prevent her getting into trouble. Extending (retractable or flexi) leads are generally not a good tool to use, as they are too bulky, and not very easy to use if you need to get your dog back to you quickly. By their very nature, there is always pressure on the lead, which is not what you want when teaching LLW!

Having a play session with your dog *before* going for a walk may help to release any excess energy and frustration, therefore making walking calmly with you that bit easier. However, you don't want to have your dog in an excitable state just before you leave the house.

You'll need to think of on lead walks as training games rather than exercise while training is on-going. Keep the sessions short (around five minutes at a time) so she can concentrate and not get bored. Until she is good at walking without pulling, it may be an idea to drive her to somewhere she can go off lead for her exercise.

We are looking for it to become more fun and rewarding to walk on a loose lead than it is to pull on the lead.

Unless you are going to compete in obedience, you can teach your dog to walk on either side of you. You can lay good foundations for on lead walking by starting without a lead. Start off in the garden where there are little in the way of distractions. Every time your dog chooses to place herself by your left leg (or right leg if that's the side you choose to walk her), click (or use a marker word, such as 'Yes') and treat. Take a pace away, then when she places herself next to you again, click and treat. Repeat several times. Once she is choosing to place herself there regularly, you can add a spoken cue when she does so. The word(s) you choose are not important but should always be the same to avoid confusion. You could use 'heel', 'close' or 'let's go' for instance.

Once you have established a foundation that being by your side is a good place to be, you can add the lead and start to walk. Start with your dog in place by your heel, and then take one pace forward. You dog should follow you, so click and treat. Then take two paces forward. Click and treat if she comes with you and does not pull on the lead. Then take three paces forward… and so on until you have built duration up to around 50 paces. At this point, if your dog is doing well, you can start to build the duration in larger increments before clicking and treating and jump to increasing by around five paces each time.

If at any time your dog starts to lose concentration or begins to pull, then you will need to reduce the number of paces you take before clicking and treating. Perhaps even start from the beginning again at one pace.

You should aim to keep preparations for going for a walk calm and low key. If your dog is bouncing around before you even leave the house, then this behaviour is likely to continue when you go out of the door. If she is bouncing around when you pick up her lead, simply put the lead down again until she is calm. Repeat if necessary until she stays calm while you pick up the lead and attach it. She will soon learn that she needs to be calm if she wants to go out for a walk. You don't need to click and treat this, as her reward will be that she gets to go for a walk.

You can also pick her lead up several times a day, but then go and do something else. This will teach her that just because you have picked up the lead, you won't necessarily be going for a walk, and should result in her not becoming overexcited every time you pick up her lead.

You need to have a large supply of treats ready for when you leave the house, either in a pocket or a treat bag where they are easily accessible. Before moving off, you need to have your dog in the correct position by your left (or right) leg. Reward her for being there by a click and treat. If she doesn't put herself in the right position even when you wait for her to do so, you can drop a treat by your left (or right) heel.

The lead and clicker should be in the hand on the opposite side to your dog. You can then use the hand nearest your dog to deliver the treat. You want to deliver the treat so that your dog stays in the correct position to doubly reinforce it, so your hand should be near your trouser seam and at your dog's head height. Using the other hand to deliver the treat may result in your dog coming across in front of you in anticipation of receiving the treat.

You need to start off in a place with few distractions and build up gradually to busier and more exciting places.

You can try several changes of direction and a change of pace to keep your dog interested and focused on you.

Try varying your treats so that sometimes they are tasty and other times they are less so, such as kibble. This will keep her interest as this time it may be something good!

Remember, training is supposed to be fun for all involved and should always end on a positive note.

Tools that may Help

While you are teaching your dog to walk on a loose lead, it may be of use to use some sort of tool so that she can still get exercise without being rewarded for pulling. I find using a flat collar with a harness, or a harness with a front and back clip, combined with a double-ended training lead (sometimes called a police lead) a good combination that manages pulling without being painful for either your dog or you!

Problems?

If your dog really isn't paying attention to you while out on a walk, she may be finding the distractions too great or may be overstimulated. If so, you could try:

- Increasing the value of the treats you are using. Try something that she finds irresistible and doesn't get at any other time.
- Going back to a quieter environment to work on her loose lead walking and gradually build up to a more distracting environment.
- You may be building the duration by too large an increment. Try going back a few stages and building increments one pace at a time.

Teaching a Dog to Walk on a Lead
By Sally Bradbury

Although this is aimed at puppies, it can also be used for adult dogs.

At his mealtimes, walk around the house and the garden holding his food bowl and give him his food one piece at a time from your other hand any time he is there beside you. This is done without a lead. Continue to do this until he understands the game and follows you about or walks with you for the whole of his meal.

Meanwhile, use some yummy treats, sit on the floor, touch his collar, and give him a treat. Repeat, repeat, repeat. Put a finger under his collar, give him a treat, and let go of his collar. Repeat, repeat, repeat. Hold his collar longer, give him a treat, and let go of his collar. Repeat, repeat, repeat. Hold his collar, attach his lead, give him a treat, hold his collar, take off his lead, and give him a treat. You get the picture.

Now, next mealtime, attach his lead to his collar, which he is now fine about. Tuck your end of the lead into your belt loop and walk around the house and garden, feeding as you go. The same as you did before, but this time, with the lead attached. Voila! Puppy walking on a loose lead.

NOTE: while a collar is referred to throughout this article, a harness is recommended once you start taking your dog out for a walk.
See: *General Advice before you Start*.

Chapter 8

Barking

Reasons for Excessive Barking
And how to fix it
By Sally Bradbury

Dogs bark for many reasons; they might be scared, surprised, alerted, happy, excited, sad, lonely, or may be communicating another emotional state.

For Alert Barking or any barking that is a reaction to a trigger, be that the dog next door, neighbours in the garden, cats, chickens, an animal on the TV, someone walking past the window, birds flying overhead in the garden, or traffic on your walk, you can play *Click the Trigger*.

You'll need a clicker (or you can use a verbal marker such as 'Yes!'), a pot of treats, and your dog on lead. You are going to need him to want to eat, so have something delicious and smelly like cooked liver or hot dog sausage. You may want to do a couple of sessions of simple clicker training first, so he knows the game.

He'll need to be under threshold, so position yourselves close enough to the trigger so that he can see or hear it, but far enough away so that he is unlikely to react.

Using traffic as an example trigger, the ideal training spot would be on a footpath or a very quiet road that leads to a minor road at a T-Junction, or a quiet corner of a supermarket car park. The traffic needs to be going across your view from left to right or right to left, not coming towards you. Ideally, it should be just one vehicle at a time, with at least a few seconds between them but preferably more.

If your dog is barking or lunging and trying to chase vehicles, you need to stay away from roads for now and walk him in traffic-free places. This may mean driving somewhere for exercise but will ensure that he isn't practising the behaviour.

Find the distance where he can see a car and not react other than noticing it. You need him on lead, some small, yummy treats, and your clicker.

Stage One
Watch his body language; you are looking for the slightest ear prick. When he notices a car, you are going to click. If you have put in the groundwork with the clicker, if he knows there are yummy treats on offer, and if you are far enough away from the traffic, then he will turn back to you for the

treat. Step back if that makes it easier for him to turn to you, and then step forward for the next one. Repeat, repeat, repeat. He notices the car, you click, he gets a treat.

Stage Two

At some point you are going to be slow with the click and he is going to see a car, turn back to you and say, 'Oi! You forgot to click'. Click and treat that. Now you know he has got it and we can move to stage two. See a car, turn back to you, and get a click and a treat.

You will need lots of sessions in lots of locations. Always ensure that he remains below his threshold, but gradually increase criteria. Get closer to the road and practise in various locations until he can walk along the road and get the occasional reinforcement for not wanting to chase or bark at the traffic.

Barking at the TV is another good example, and this is one of the easiest triggers to control.

Sit with him on lead as far away from the TV as you can get. If necessary, move the television opposite a doorway and sit outside the room, looking in towards it. Turn the volume down to zero and use a recorded programme so that you know when to expect to see the animals or whatever will usually trigger the barking. If he is triggered by the sound of a particular advert or theme tune, then just lower the volume rather than muting it completely.

Give him one or two treats before turning on the TV to increase his motivation to work with you.

Then as soon as he sees an animal on the TV, click or say your marker word and treat. If he won't take his eyes from the screen, hit the pause button and see what happens. Your aim is for him to see something on the TV that he would normally bark at, but instead to turn to you for a treat.

You'll need to experiment a bit. If you click and he still barks, he still gets the treat. A click is always a promise of a reward. Once you can sit far away from the TV and he can see an animal and immediately turn to you and say 'I saw that dog/cat/meerkat. Treat please', then you very gradually up the ante. Add some volume, move closer. If it goes wrong at any time, go back two stages and get that stage perfect again.

Meanwhile, you'll need to avoid all instances of letting him practise the behaviour you are trying to eliminate. Otherwise, it will take a long time to make any progress. You may have to make sacrifices and read instead of watching TV, or watch when he isn't in the room.

You Can Use the Same Method for Anything that triggers barking. If it's a dog on the other side of the fence, then sit away from the fence with him. Watch him closely; click and treat when his ears prick at hearing something. You may have to start indoors with the door open or as far from the fence as you can be in the garden. Don't let him spend time in the garden alone; take him out on lead unless you have an arrangement with the neighbours and your dogs on a rota. As you progress, you can lengthen the lead, so he has to return to you for the treat after hearing/seeing the trigger. Eventually, he can be off lead and play training games with you instead of barking at the dog next door.

For People, Dogs, Wildlife, or anything passing the house when your dog is indoors, you can work in a similar way. If it's noises, then sit on the far side of the front room. If it's visual, then be in a position where he can see out, but you can retreat if needed. Meanwhile, use blinds or window film, or close the door to that room when you are not in there.

Cats don't tend to cooperate, so you'll need another person to help. See: *Cats and Small Furries, Teaching Tolerance.*

Chickens must be enclosed and kept as far away as needed.

Barking at Birds in Flight or Squirrels in the garden can also be dealt with by playing click the trigger. Work with your dog outdoors but near the door so you can retreat indoors if necessary.

Attention Seeking Barking is best resolved by giving the dog attention before he has to ask for it. Contrary to popular belief, ignoring a dog that has a genuine need just makes them try harder. It's very frustrating and stressful for a dog that is trying to communicate with you.

Make sure his needs are met. If he isn't hungry, has water, doesn't need to go out for a pee, has had a walk, then he may simply need your attention, just as a toddler would. If he's persistently barking for attention, it may be necessary to assess your dog's routine. Does he have enough enrichment in his daily routine? Is he able to relax when everyone else is? See: *The Lounge is for Lounging.*

Teaching a dog to bark on cue so you can teach a 'quiet' is often suggested, but not something we would recommend. Rewarding a dog for stopping an unwanted behaviour sounds fine in theory, but in practise the dog must do the behaviour first in order to stop. It's always best to reward the absence of the barking.

If Your Dog Barks When You're Trying to Eat

When you sit down to eat, have a bowl of treats available for him and a strategically placed bed by your feet, under the table, or across the room. *Before* he barks, toss a treat onto his bed for him and continue to do this at a pace that keeps him on his bed and not barking. If there are two of you, then it would be a good idea to eat in shifts so that one person can concentrate on teaching him to stay on his bed while you eat. This will only be necessary in the beginning.

The Two-Second Time-Out

This is the only time-out that we recommend. Anything longer, and learning doesn't happen. It's just punishment.

Let's use playing ball as a popular example. Dog barks in excitement as he wants the ball thrown. If you throw the ball, he's learning to bark. If you don't throw the ball, he's getting frustrated. Eventually, you either throw the ball, or he just tries harder and harder because barking always works.

It's all in the timing. Find a way to throw the ball before he barks. You could drop the ball on the floor while his lead is still on, then remove the lead and move the ball with your toe. His head is down, and he doesn't bark. You could then drop some food on the floor. As he finishes the food, throw the ball. If he brings the ball back, throw it again immediately before he barks. Not possible? Throw a second ball while the first one is still in his mouth. Continue in this fashion, getting the ball to him so quickly that he just doesn't bark. To teach him not to bark at all, start to pause slightly before throwing the ball – just a nano-second. If he doesn't bark, throw the ball. If he barks, step away, turn around, and reset for two seconds max. Throw the ball if the barking has stopped. This delays the reward and says to the dog, 'You got it wrong, try again'.

NOTE: we don't recommend lots of ball throwing, but it's an easy example to use for attention seeking barking.

Prevention of Unwanted Barking

By Emma Judson

Dogs bark for a reason. Probably several reasons. Until you find that reason and eliminate it, it will continue.

Using punishment may have a slight, short-term effect. It won't work long-term because punishment merely suppresses a behaviour. It does not actually address the root cause, so the behaviour will come back.

This is a bit like sticking a big ole plaster on a festering wound. Sure, you can't see the wound anymore, but it's still there. It isn't going to get better just because the plaster is hiding it. It is only going to get worse.

Dogs bark to communicate. They may want to tell you they heard something, or to tell the thing they heard to go away. They may bark because barking is inherently enjoyable to do, because they are overexcited or stressed, or because they are fearful. They may possibly bark for several of these reasons combined.

Boredom

Barking is fun! Make sure your dogs are getting the physical and mental exercise they need. If they have no issues with going for walks on a lead, then take them for a couple of walks a day. They can also play games, solve puzzles, eat food from toys (such as Kongs), search for their scattered food, and, of course, do training sessions with you.

Make sure that the activities you do are not all very high energy, whizzy things. Limit activities like going for walks where they yell at everything they see, chasing a ball endlessly, or hurtling around with other dogs. A little bit of those things is fine, but a lot of it is just going to create lots of stress. Like kids at a fairground, they get wound up and can't unwind.

Try to organise your daily routine so that any high energy stuff is followed by calming stuff. For example, a clicker training session can be quite an exciting activity, so follow it up with a calming activity, like sniffing outdoors for scattered kibble.

Barking at Sounds

This is best addressed by counter-conditioning. Put simply, click (or mark) and treat any sound you hear. Do not wait for the dogs to bark, do not tell them to be quiet; just pair the sound with a high-value reward like a little cube of cheese or sausage. You will need to walk around for a week or two with a full treat pouch whenever you are home. Alternatively, you could keep treats in pots or dishes in every room out of your dog's reach, so that when you hear a sound you can say 'Yes!' and grab them all a goodie.

Over time, this teaches them that sounds/sights = treats, and any fearful or reactive desire to bark fades away.

Barking at Sounds that are Exciting

Excited barking includes barking at the postal delivery or the doorbell and can be dealt with systematically.

Start by disconnecting the doorbell and putting a note with your phone number on the door asking folk to phone you rather than knock. If your dog is reacting to post coming through the letter box/slot in the door, replace it with an external box.

Then you have the space you need to re-teach your dogs that, for example, the sound of the doorbell means 'you will get a treat if you sit', or 'go to your bed for a treat'. You can get a new doorbell so that it has a brand-new sound. There are wireless options with a remote bell push, which means that you will be able to activate the doorbell yourself from indoors. Effectively, the sound is taught as a cue to do something, just as the word 'sit' means 'park your butt'. It takes a while, particularly with multiple dogs, but it can be done.

If you find the sound of the postal delivery or a visitor coming through a gate sets your dog off, you can counter-condition this in the same way as scary sounds. Pair the sound with the reward until their automatic reaction is not to bark but to look at you for their reward.

Doing the things outlined above should really help to reduce the barking. It's important to avoid shouting at them; it just sounds as if you are joining in!

It's also really important to note that when you are counter-conditioning, the dogs get a treat when you hear the sound. The reward is not dependent on them behaving well or keeping quiet. They will start to keep quiet as their need to bark reduces!

Very often, people tell me that counter-conditioning doesn't work. What I then see is people hearing a sound, and then waiting for the dog to make a mistake – to bark – and then telling the dog to be quiet! That isn't counter-conditioning!

Even if you hear a sound and your dogs bark before you can give them a treat, you still need to treat them. You will not be rewarding bad behaviour by doing so. Frankly, even if they did then learn to bark to get a treat, that is far more easily resolved than barking out of fear or anxiety!

Chapter 9

Dogs and Babies

Preparing your Dog for the Arrival of a Baby

By Rebecca Köhnke

When you find out that you're expecting, you have a gazillion things on your mind.

It's important to consider the family dog in this situation, too. A lot of things are going to change. If you use the pregnancy to prepare him for what's coming, then life will be a lot easier when things get real. This is particularly relevant for parents expecting their first baby, or their first baby with a new dog. (Apologies, gents, for talking to the ladies a lot in some passages. Don't feel left out. It's just difficult to keep this gender neutral. Our example dog will be a boy though!)

So, sit down for a few minutes and think about the following issues:

- What sort of dog do you have?
- Is he pretty unflappable or easily stressed?
- Does he like children or is he rather worried by them?
- Has he met babies at all?
- How does he deal with change?
- Does he need a fixed routine? Or does he not mind if the days are all a bit here, there, and everywhere?
- Is he young and energetic? Or maybe old and sore?
- How attached is he to the adults in the family?
- How much attention does he need?
- What cues does he know? Does he know them reliably?
- What sort of things worry you when you think about your dog living together with a baby?

Each family is different, and so is every dog. Be honest, and possibly a bit over-critical, rather than blasé about these questions. The answers will help you determine how you should be preparing.

Now, seeing as I've just recently been through this myself with two very different dogs and two very different babies, let me give you a bit of an idea of what is likely to change.

Let's start in pregnancy. You'll become, well, round. Walrus-shaped, it'll feel like. You won't be able to cuddle your dogs as comfortably. You might feel hot all the time and not enjoy a canine radiator right close to you. Sooner or later, you will become short of breath, and most likely tired, too. So, walks will become slower, shorter, and flatter.

You might be incapacitated for a period of your pregnancy. You might even have to stay in hospital for a while.

In most cases, you will have to go to hospital in the end, most probably rather spontaneously, and you may have to stay for a bit.

While you are preparing for the baby, you will quite likely undertake some renovating or redecorating. You might even move house. New furniture will appear and/or need to be built, possibly using power tools. Equipment such as a pram, nappy bin, or a car seat will arrive. Some of these car seats double as a rocker. My dog found tapping it with their nose or paw to make it move hilarious! You might have the midwife come round and possibly examine you at home. You'll go on parental leave, be home a lot, go to the doctor's a lot, then suddenly disappear, possibly at an ungodly hour, and your dog may be left home alone.

So, now you're new parents, and about to bring home your little bundle. You'll carry them in your arms or bring them in in the car seat.

They will sometimes be asleep and sometimes awake. They'll eventually burst into song. They might do that a lot, even. They will trap you under them when they've fallen asleep, and you won't really want to move; if you're lucky, you'll be able to stay put for a few hours. And chances are, at least for the first few weeks, you'll have no idea when those naps are going to happen. If you're really lucky, you can at some point actually put the baby down for a nap. So, you'll put up a baby monitor. Which, at some point, will start blaring this really weird sounding cry.

The baby will sigh, squeak, whine, mumble, and even breathe. One of my dogs had a meltdown after my first baby arrived because the travel cot suddenly made breathing sounds.

You'll be spending weeks to months, depending on the character of your baby, trying to find your feet. You'll be doing everything the way that the baby needs it, when the baby needs it done; you'll be accommodating every need your baby has, which will change every couple of weeks. It's basically a game of ever-changing goal posts.

You might have someone home with you for a while. You might be fit and healthy in no time, or you might be unwell, injured or need to rest.

Your health visitor will stop by a lot.

Other people may want to stop by a lot.

At some point, you'll fall back into some sort of normality. You'll be used to doing everything with one hand and always keeping Baby close. You'll be taking them to the bathroom with you and sitting on the floor with them for playtime. You'll start to venture out, even with the dogs. You might want to take them all in the car, or you might want to push Baby in the pram. You might have stairs to negotiate or muddy paws to clean before letting your dog in the house.

Sooner than you think, your baby will be interactive and even mobile. They'll scream, shout, squeal, hiccup, flail their arms and legs, and throw things. Then they will start to roll; some only roll over, others roll right across the room. Your baby is now mobile and will make its own way along the floor. It'll investigate everything; sleeping dogs, empty or occupied dog beds, water and food bowls (!!!), toys of any variety. You name it. You'll need to pre-empt and prevent, of course, because they'll definitely try if they get the chance.

Then not long after, they'll start pulling themselves up. On you, on the table, on whatever they can find. Again, this includes dogs in any and all positions and situations. No, Baby shouldn't be allowed that – but they sure will try!

The next step after that, of course, is moving on two legs. Unsteadily at first, unpredictably, and unable to be careful. Also, somewhat vulnerable to falling if knocked by more than a feather.

And that's just the first year. Chances are, at some point, Mum will be going back to work and not be home as much anymore. A childminder or relative might even be in the house instead.

Now, I've told you all this, and I've not even mentioned what to do with your dog.

True.

Because to a degree, it'll be different for every family. Look at that text again. Think about how your dog would handle each of these developments; what he might do and how he might react.

That will give you a good idea of what you need to consider when preparing your dog for the new arrival.

A few general things will need to be considered in nearly all cases:

- Look at your dog's **exercise needs.** How will you be able to meet them? Are you over-fulfilling them so far? Frequently doing activities, going on strenuous hikes? It might be a good idea to gradually reduce them, as you may well not be able to keep them up for a while
- Think about your **routine.** This will basically go out the window for a while as far as the dogs are concerned. If they have a set schedule, now is the time to start slowly and gradually varying it by ten, fifteen, twenty minutes back and forth, building up until the schedule is gone
- How about **beds and sleeping arrangements?** Where do the dogs sleep now? Will this stay the same after Baby is born? Will their beds be in a convenient space, so you don't trip over them at night when getting up? Will they have a safe space that Baby can't get to, even once they are mobile? How can you ensure this as the baby develops?
- Now consider your **rooms and access** to those spaces. Which rooms are they allowed in now? Which ones do you want them in later? Which ones will be off limits? Start teaching that now. Not only is it much easier for all of you, but it'll also prevent him forming negative associations with the baby
- **Food and water bowls** are favourite crawler targets. Find an inaccessible space! This is important! A dog should not have to worry about a child interfering with their food and drink. It is, of course, particularly important if your dog has a history of guarding food or water
- Put some thought into **child and dog safety.** How does your dog feel about a baby close by? Direct contact should be avoided. But can he cope with Baby in the same room? Will they leave if they have had enough? Can he have toys without the baby getting them? Where can the baby hang out with toys without the dogs interfering? Sometimes, you will need both of your hands; how will you then keep both Baby and your dog safe and happy, and avoid risking any incidents or accidents? Stairgates, playpens, and crates can all be useful here
- You will also need to consider **traffic safety.** Has your dog ever seen a pram? Can he walk beside one? Can you negotiate curbs, corners, and stairs in this setup? Can you get the baby and dogs in and out of the car safely?

- **Where do you want your dog to be** and what do you want your dog to be able to do? As mentioned above, think about where their beds should be, reinforce them strongly for using as their safe spots. Make these a preferred place now. Rooms that are off limits rooms can be gated off or you put a mat just outside them and teach a default down on that, although this is a lot less reliable. Do you need to practise a cue to direct your dog on and off furniture? Do you need to refresh recall, loose lead walking, or polite behaviour in doorways? Do this now!

In addition to these general areas, there will be specific issues that each individual dog may struggle with.

Does your dog do well with change? If not, consider spreading out the decorating and furniture building to give him time to adjust. Plan to finish early enough to allow him time to get comfortable with the full setup, including the pram, car seat and other seemingly superficial changes. Also, if you'll be using baby toiletries, consider using them on yourself for a few weeks before the baby arrives, so the dog can get used to the smell and associate it with you.

Is your dog not good with strangers or guests? Think about how to manage this; practise him being put away in a safe room with a nice chew, or practise polite greetings.

Is your dog noise sensitive? Play some baby sounds from YouTube while doing nice things. Start at a very low volume and gradually work your way up.

Not sure how your dog will react if you're holding something in your arms? Get yourself a baby doll and try. If it can cry, that will help you gauge how they would react to strange and sudden noises from your arms, too. Practise when you are standing up and also sitting down. It won't be the perfect double for your baby, but it'll give you an idea of whether you need to work on this. Plus, it'll demonstrate to you how life will be with only one free hand. It's quite an eye opener.

Baby wearing can be a great, practical solution to many everyday issues while keeping Baby safe, comfortable, and out of trouble. You can rent or borrow a carrier, wrap, or sling and use your doll to make your dog familiar with long bits of fabric dangling or being tied, rings clattering or buckles clicking. This is also a chance to get him used to you moving slightly awkwardly for short periods of time. The bonus is that you'll already be familiar with your chosen carrier when Baby gets involved!

You will need to make arrangements in case you will be away from home for the birth or unable to walk the dog during or after pregnancy. Who will take care of your dog? Who will come into the house and pick him up or let him out if you need to leave quickly? Who will take him for walks? Introduce these people now and make sure that your dog will be okay with them.

If your dog is overly attached to one of you, it might be a good idea to start introducing a visual unavailability cue.
See: *Hatting* for help with this.

By now, you'll have realised that there will be different areas of work for each family. The following tips might also help you:

- A Pet Remedy or Adaptil diffuser plugged in a few weeks ahead may make it easier for some dogs
- Avoid the dreaded visitor rush for everyone's sake
- Ask friends and family for help with the dog if the dog is comfortable with that
- Make yourself dog-savvy! Learn as much as possible about their body language! This will help you loads in assessing situations as they arise!
- Make sure the dog still gets individual attention
- Don't only give attention when Baby is asleep, as the dog may quickly learn 'Baby awake means no time for me', which may not be a good thing
- Bring a piece of Baby's clothing back from the hospital before Baby arrives home, but don't worry about introducing the dog and Baby formally; he knows the baby is there!

Pram Training
By Rebecca Köhnke

1. Put your pram/buggy up somewhere where your dog can see and investigate it, but where he has plenty space to go elsewhere without having to go past the buggy. This could be inside or in the garden, but should be calm and without any distractions.
2. Get yourself a large treat pouch or bowl. This should by filled with lots and lots of small treats; very small cheese cubes are good for this if your dog likes them.
3. Sit near the pram with your treats in reach, but not in your hand. Your dog can just roam. Whenever your dog shows interest in the pram, click or mark and toss a treat just behind him. Being able to increase distance to the new object is a reward in and of itself, and a very

valuable one at that. For obvious reasons, don't reward exuberant or inquisitive actions, such as paw swatting, biting, or climbing the pram.

4. You'll notice your dog becoming more comfortable around the pram. That's what you want; comfortable, not mega-excited, crazy, happy, or bouncing.

5. With your dog still loose, handle and fold the pram several times. Again, tossing treats behind the dog as you go. Watch for signs that the dog is comfortable, not excited.

6. Next, move the pram back and forward a bit, lift the front and/or back as if trying to negotiate corners and curbs. Toss treats as before. Again, comfortable is your goal.

7. Think about which side you want your dog to be on. I like him to be on the side which is furthest from the traffic. Now we'll get moving. Take your treats with you; keep them easy to reach, but not in your hand.

8. Slowly push the buggy. Whenever your dog happens to be at the side you picked, mark and treat. I like to treat on the floor at this point, on my chosen side, at about my 7 o'clock position, as the floor serves to automatically 'reset' the dog. You could treat from your hand instead, if you prefer, from slightly behind your thigh. What I'm doing here, is making 'beside and slightly behind me' the sweet spot. I want the dog to be slightly behind, so that later, neither he, nor the lead, can get caught under the wheels.

9. Soon, you'll notice that the dog will come right back to his sweet spot after he's finished eating. That's fab!

10. Now throw in some bends and curves. While doing so, make sure to treat often in that 'slightly behind and beside' position. This ensures that the dog learns not to rush in front when you're going around bends. Include inward turns, too; these are tricky!

11. When your dog happily stays in their sweet spot, regardless of what direction or speed you're going, it's time to add the lead. Keep going with your treats as before; best from your hand now as your dog won't now be able to stop and sniff out treats. Repeat all your moves with the lead on.

12. Keep rewarding that sweet spot every so often to keep it to keep it reinforced!

13. Give a release cue to let your dog go when off lead.

Done! Now you can add a cue. For my dogs, the presence of the pram and putting the lead on is cue enough.

Take it outdoors in increasingly difficult environments. Think about how to best negotiate leaving and returning to your home and teach this. Don't forget to factor in stairs. For example, I have two large dogs, a three-foot-wide, six-foot-long hallway with three steep steps leading outdoors, and a pretty large pram. I get the pram out first, then fetch the dogs from the living room. Reverse on entry, or the pram just stays in the garage. It pays to do this with an empty pram first, maybe with a baby doll. It'll be a lot to handle at first for both you and your dog, so be sure to get comfortable before Baby is actually there.

If you think a situation might be too difficult, either turn away, or move to the side. Then secure the pram, move the dog to the back or front of the pram, and away to the side. That way, they can't knock it over if something puts him over threshold and they jump.

If you have more than one dog, practise with each of them separately, and then join them up. I like mine to both be on the same side when on lead. They also have their set order of who's closer to and who's further away from me. I keep that when out with the pram.

Chapter 10

The Multi-Pet Household

Living in a Multi-Dog Household
By Sally Bradbury

Living in a multi-dog household has its challenges, and we'll address some of them here.

Always have more resting places or beds than you have dogs. Teach all dogs to go to a bed or crate on cue. If you have two dogs that are sometimes a little antsy with each other, then make sure that you can send those two to a bed or crate in two different directions to diffuse any potential conflict.

All of the exercises detailed below will go a long way to avoiding trigger points that lead to conflict. Resource guarding of food, toys, and resting places is the most common cause for conflict, as well as competition for your attention.

Don't feel that all dogs need to be treated in the same way if they all have different requirements and motivations. A youngster will need a lot more attention, more meals, and more trips to the garden, for example.

Sometimes, despite all our best efforts, dogs that live together may fall out. Ritualised aggression, aka handbags at dawn, is harmless, but if two dogs fight and cause injury to each other, then separate them. Be sure to get them both a health check, as well as seeing to the war wounds. Occasionally, an older dog will be the target when he is losing his faculties and becoming deaf/blind. This is the time to give him somewhere safe, away from the younger dog.

If two dogs fall out big time and a medical cause has been ruled out, you may have to accept that the relationship has broken down to the point where they will need to live separately. It's possible they may be able to live separately under the same roof, but only if strict management can be maintained.

Whether you have two dogs or ten, you'll need to follow some simple rules to ensure harmony and avoid conflicts.

Getting a New Dog

Ideally, leave a gap of 18 months when getting a second puppy, so that the first puppy has gone through puppyhood, adolescence, and successfully come out the other side. Then you can start all over again with puppy number two, and three, and so on!

If you are adopting adult dogs, then leave a sensible gap between them so that they have time to settle in and bond with you before you introduce a new dog.

It's important that the new dog/puppy and the existing dog are introduced slowly and that both are given as much individual attention as possible, preferably with one adult per dog.
See: also *Introducing a New Puppy to the Family Dog(s)* and *Bringing Home a New Dog*.

Always feed the dogs separately; if possible, in two different rooms. Do this even if they are fine eating together and like to swap bowls or lick each other's bowls when they are finished. They will only be fine until they aren't, so it's not worth the risk. The only reason to feed dogs together is if you want to practise breaking up dog fights!

It's good to give them separate walks, so that the new dog/puppy bonds with you on walks, and you can work on nice lead walking and recall. This is especially important if your older dog is reactive, runs off, or pulls on the lead. This avoids him influencing the puppy until after your training and influence has been established. Besides, they will have different exercise requirements in the early days.

Roll Call

Teach all dogs to respond to their name and their name only. This ensures that you can call an individual dog to you without them all coming at once. You can have a collective name if you want them to respond together.

You can teach them this **using food.** Start off by saying each dog's name as you hand out treats. If you already have more than two dogs, work in each combination of pairs, and then threes, and so on. The advanced stage of this exercise would involve you holding a meat roasting tin for each dog to lick, one at a time. Call one forward, tell him to finish and go back, then call the next one. This will require a lot of individual training, building up gradually to pairs, and then continuing just as you did when handing out treats.

Another good way to teach each dog their name is through **play and training**. Start this with each dog individually. The idea is that each dog will be able to work/play without being distracted by the other dog(s). Conflict over or resource guarding a toy can be avoided by making sure each dog has their own toy during play/training sessions.

- **Stage One**
  Teach each dog to only go after their toy when you say their name. So, take each dog outdoors separately, say their name, and throw their toy. Repeat many times
- **Stage Two**
  Slowly toss a boring toy and immediately say the dog's name while throwing the exciting toy in the other direction
- **Stage Three**
  Say the other dog's name with the boring throw, then immediately say the dog's name while throwing the exciting toy in the other direction

When each dog can ignore the thrown toy when you say the other dog's name and only goes after the one on their name, then you take them both out together with a toy each. The toys can be identical or they can be different, if they both have a different favourite.

Now with Dog A on lead, or with you holding his harness or collar, gently throw Dog B's toy for him, and then Dog A's in the other direction. Repeat until both dogs are only interested their own toy.

Once you have two dogs doing this, it will be a doddle with the third, fourth and fifth dogs. Make sure all the dogs have a favourite toy that is theirs alone.

Training sessions with food or toys are easy once you have taught each individual dog to stay on a mat, go to a crate, or settle and wait at a different station. Every time the dog being trained gets a reward, so does the spectator for staying put and watching nicely until it's his turn.

Going through doors and gates

Start by teaching each dog individually. Choose a door that the dog wants to go through and that opens away from you for the initial training. Open the door a crack, say nothing. If he moves forward, close the door. Repeat until he doesn't move, then open the door wide as you give a release cue. For multi-dog families, the best release cue is the dog's name.

Next session, open the door slightly wider and, as before, open and close it until he pauses. Open it half an inch more until he waits or pauses, then open the door, release him, and allow him through the door.

Continue in this fashion until he waits in front of a wide-open door for the cue to go through.

When they can all do this, begin training in pairs. Start this phase with one dog on lead, and only release the off-lead dog to go through the door. Practise in pairs, then threes, and then start again at other doors and gates until the behaviour is generalised.

If you consistently do this at certain doors and gates each day, then your dog(s) will wait to go through until released without being asked. If you are not consistent, then you will need to introduce the wait cue so that your dog knows when they have to wait and when they don't. I would recommend making this a default behaviour at external doors.

One Dog Good. Seven Dogs Better?
By Emma Judson

I have almost always had multiple dogs. Personally, it's the right thing for me and my dogs, but there are some things that you should know.

Don't get a second dog expecting that they will be the first dog's best friend. Dogs have evolved to want to spend time with us. While I firmly believe they should spend time with other dogs, the chances of us choosing another dog who turns out to be someone they adore – well, that's going to require a lot of luck!

If you do get a second dog who loves and wants to play with your other dog all the time, then that can actually be pretty annoying to live with. Constant rough and tumble dog play is filled with risk in much the same way as children running around, yelling and chasing is. Someone's going to fall over and there will be tears! The risk of arguments, injuries, actual fights, or grudges that never pass is significant.

The best reason to get another dog is because you want one and have the time, patience, funds and space to have one, two, or five dogs.

More than one dog means triple the work, or sometimes more. Everything you do with one, you must be able to do with all the others, and in any combination. You need to be able to walk not just one dog nicely on lead, but all the others, too. Dogs One and Two should be able to walk together, Dog One and Dog Three, Dog Two and Dog Three; the required behaviour must work in every combination!

Don't get a second dog to fix the first dog's behavioural or training problems. That rarely works. I hear it recommended for separation anxiety most often, but this only works if the dog is struggling with separation from another dog. When that is the case, it is usually from a specific dog who has been rehomed or who has sadly died; not 'just any old dog'.

If you already have behaviour problems with one dog, get those fixed and sorted out before you get a second dog. Some issues, such as fear, barking, reactivity, guarding food, and sound phobias can, indeed, be passed on to a second dog.

Most of my dogs would quite happily be only dogs. They like each other well enough; they play, they interact, they sometimes curl up together and share a snuggle in a warm spot. They're also all independently secure and confident, so that the loss of one will not cause serious upset in the others.

People sometimes think it is cute if two dogs are heavily dependent on one another; 'Awww, they love each other'. This dependence leads to behavioural problems. If one needs surgery and crate rest, and the other still needs walking, but neither can cope without the other, then everyone will experience stress.

Often in these 'bonded pairs', I see one dog that has no confidence at all, and the other dog is actually a bit of a bully. They have a dysfunctional relationship that isn't healthy for either of them and is not 'cute'. Rather, it's incredibly stressful for both dogs to live that way.

Consider the practicalities of more than one dog as well. Two dogs tend not to be much more work and bother than one, but three dogs, four dogs; I've had as many as seven dogs here, in what is not a particularly large house.

You can't just chuck them all in the car and go for a walk. You can't fit seven dogs into one normal sized car, but even if you could, is rocking up to the park with seven dogs fair on everyone else? Can you control all seven at once? What if one has an accident, one does a runner, and one jumps in someone else's car? You would need at least two adults – possibly more.

How about pavement walks? Well, yes, you could have seven dogs all trained nicely to walk on the lead, but that blocks up the pavement. I think it is pretty antisocial to walk such a large group of dogs down the pavement that you force others to get out of your way. It isn't good for the dogs to be walked as a gang each time, anyway. You have to be able to split them and do individual walks as well, which will take a lot of time and organisation.

Finding seven spaces to feed each dog separately in what is only a three-bedroom house was challenging. Finding seven spaces for each to eat a chew, or finding a separate place to train while the other six relaxed, wasn't easy either.

Fortunately, I only had seven for a few months. Then we were back to five. Even so, five dogs are more than most people have. It raises eyebrows, heart rates, and bills.

The cost

Even when my kind vet only charges me one consultation fee, five sets of flea treatments and five sets of wormers mean a regular cost of hundreds of pounds rather than forty or fifty.

Food

I have a separate freezer for dog food. Although I get a bulk order deal from the food supplier, that still means driving to them to collect it monthly rather than picking it up in the local pet store. If I fed dry food, I could get that delivered, but a month's worth of dry food for five dogs can take up a fair whack of space.

Insurance

While some will do a discount on multiple pets, it isn't much. Insurance for several dogs is a significant outlay.

Holidays

Sitters, kennels, and boarders all cost more with each pet. If you want to take your dogs with you, you will find that one or two dogs are easy to accommodate, but when you get to three or more, things get much harder.

What if it all goes wrong?

When we bring a new dog home to our existing dog, or our group of dogs, we can never be certain that they will get along. Any new addition changes the dynamic within the group. We won't know for sure if it's all working out nicely for probably a year or two, once that new dog is fully grown and settled in.

If it goes wrong, we could have scraps, arguments, or serious fights. Heck, when it's going *right*, we can still have the odd 'handbags' moment, or the occasional misunderstanding. We may have to separate a particular combination of dogs permanently or consider rehoming someone.

These are not pleasant things to think about, but if you want to have a multi-dog household, you really must think about these issues in advance.

When it all works out, though, when everyone gets on and shares the space nicely, there is nothing nicer than putting your feet up in front of the fire and having a pile of dogs draped across your lap, feet, and shoulders. Well, until someone needs to get up for a wee!

Bringing Home a New Dog
By Jo Maisey

The following is applicable whether your new dog is a temporary foster or a permanent addition, regardless of whether he is from a shelter, a breeder, or anywhere else.

Introduction

Many dogs can meet each other for the first time and get along fantastically. However, if initial introductions are not made correctly, there is the potential for it all to go horribly wrong. It is much better to predict, prevent, and avoid a potential problem, than to create a problem that you will then need to fix by counter-conditioning. It is not realistic to expect dogs to get thrown together in an unfamiliar environment and to be able to seamlessly adapt. At best, one or both dogs may feel anxious. At worst, there could be a trip to the vet. It is particularly important that the introductions go well.

Most dogs experience some level of stress when they arrive at a new location. Even if they were friendly, bouncy, playful dogs before, the transition to a new environment can be a very frightening time for a dog, and he may behave in a very different manner than when you first met him.

Before You Bring Home Your New Dog

Ensure your home is set up to avoid conflict:

- Pick up and put away all food
- Pick up and put away all toys
- Pick up and put away all chews, bones, and similar items
- Have crates, beds and baby gates set up ready
- Have a plan in mind of which dog will go where and how you will manage feeding, toileting and walking
- Ensure there are enough water bowls in various parts of the house

What to do When you Arrive Home

Even the most well-balanced dog will feel a little anxious about entering an unknown environment. They don't know you, the house, the neighbourhood, the house rules, or what is expected of them. In order to avoid potential conflict between resident and new dogs:

- Don't allow the dogs to meet initially. While it is likely that they have met previously to gauge how they will get along together, taking them home changes the environment
- Don't simply throw the dogs in together and hope for the best
- Don't assume that they will 'sort themselves out'. The potential is there for some severe damage to one or more dogs. Don't set them up to fail!
- Don't feed them together. Resource guarding is a natural behaviour for a dog. Don't make him feel the need to do it
- Don't give either or both dogs anything they may feel the need to defend, such as chews or toys, unless they are safely away from the other dog(s)
- Do keep the dogs separated by using crates, baby gates, or separate rooms
- Do feed them in separate rooms and pick up empty bowls as soon as possible
- Do prepare all food while the dogs are separated
- Do ensure all the dogs have easy access to water

Making the Introductions

Once your new dog seems to be more relaxed and settled, you can think about introducing him to the resident dog(s). It's likely that this may be after a day or two, but some dogs may need longer than others to settle. Some new dogs will slot in as if they have always lived there, and so both will be happy together after a few hours. Be guided by your dogs' behaviour.

Think first

If you do not have confidence in your skills, there is a big size difference between the dogs, or one of the dogs has previously shown aggression, it may be better for you to enlist the help of a force-free behaviourist/trainer.

Ensure you have at least one other adult with you

You need to have at least one other adult with you in case of a problem. Ideally, this should be someone who can read canine body language and have the skills to calmly intervene if necessary. Let them know exactly what your plans are and what you need them to do.

Do not have children with you when you are doing introductions.

Introduce dogs on neutral ground

This is especially important if one or more of your dogs tends to be territorial. A securely enclosed area where you can control the environment would be ideal.

Introduce dogs outdoors

There is less likely to be a territorial issue outdoors, and if there is, everyone has plenty of space to move away. There are no corners or furniture to get trapped by.

Start with the dogs on lead and at a distance from each other

It's best to use long lines and harnesses to prevent tension on the lead.

Get one person to take the new dog a distance away from the entrance to whatever area you decide to use for introductions. Then you can bring in the resident dog (or vice versa). Start by walking both dogs parallel to each other, or play follow the leader, far enough apart so that neither dog feels the need to react, can concentrate on their handler, and can take high-value rewards.

If all is going well, gradually let them get nearer to each other with you between them until you are a few feet apart. Throughout this process, keep leads nice and loose, be interesting and rewarding, and avoid any telling off or 'correction'. We want the dogs to associate one another with low-stress, high-reward, and calm activity.

If at any stage one or both of the dogs react, increase the distance between them and get your dog's focus back on you using rewards.

When you can walk the dogs close enough to be in sniffing distance without reacting, one of you should drop back a little so your dog can sniff the other dog's butt. Keep this first greeting really short and positive. About three seconds. Then in a happy voice say, 'let's go' and return to parallel walking. Repeat a minute or so later with the other dog doing the sniffing. This allows the dogs to get used to one another without there being time for anything to go wrong.

If there is no tension and the area is safely enclosed, drop the long line so they can meet at their own speed, on their own terms, offering natural body language signals. You should continue walking so that the dogs have something to do other than fixate on each other. Recall them often before any play can get over the top. Reward well and send them back to play again. If either dog ignores the recall, use the long lines to gently put distance between them again, and get their focus back on you before allowing them back together. It's important that when this happens, *both* dogs are brought back under control. If you have one dog loose and trying to play while the other dog is secured on the lead, then that's a recipe for something to kick off.

If you are unable to drop the long line, continue with parallel walking.

The very worst way of introducing dogs is on a short lead, nose to nose. When on lead they are trapped and cannot move away as they would do naturally. Nose to nose is very rude in dog language. Polite dogs approach each other in a 'C' shape, with calming signals, such as head turns, lip licks, and sniffing the ground.

Introduce dogs one at a time

If you have more than one resident dog, introduce them one at a time to avoid overwhelming the new dog. Start with the dog least likely to cause a problem for the new dog. Once these two have been successfully introduced and are comfortable in each other's company, remove the first resident dog and introduce the next dog. Once all the resident dogs have been successfully introduced to the new dog individually, you can introduce the first two resident dogs again as a pair. Then add one more dog at a time, until all the dogs are together. If at any point one or more of the dogs are showing signs of tension, such as stiffness, trying to avoid the other dogs, growling, or snarling – STOP. You may want to do this over several days to avoid too much stress.

Minor disagreements are a way of natural communication

Raised lips, maybe a growl, snarl or snap (with no contact) is how dogs tell each other that they are not comfortable and to back off. As long as it goes no further than this and the dog on the receiving end takes notice, then this is perfectly normal. However, it would be sensible not to push the introductions any further at this point to avoid an increase in reactivity.

Intervene if appropriate

If one dog appears fearful, or there is any reactivity, then you need to step in, separate them, and create distance between them. Do not try to continue with the introductions, but go back several steps in your programme and have a rethink. Perhaps one or both dogs are not yet relaxed and settled enough to be introduced.

Remain calm

Keep your voice calm and cheerful. Move slowly. Avoid sudden movements and shouting. If you need to intervene, use a cheerful, positive voice to call and praise your dog. Avoid using any sort of punishment, including shouting and reprimands. This will only increase tension.

Remember that even though the dogs were OK together outdoors, there may still be issues indoors due to lack of space. You may need to continue your regime of separation for a while longer. Definitely avoid all potential flash points, such as food and toys.

Conclusion

If you plan things correctly from the start and set the dogs up to succeed, you are far less likely to run into problems later. It's so much easier to predict and prevent than it is to fix a problem that could have been avoided. It is always better to be overcautious!

Cats and Small Furries

By Sally Bradbury and Emma Judson

Many dogs live happily alongside cats and other animals. However, some breeds of dog, such as terriers, have generations of ancestry telling them to grab and kill small furry things. A cat's instincts are to hiss and either fight or run. Either of these behaviours is likely to wind up a dog even more.

Play between puppies and cats may look innocent, but it's possible that it's not actually innocent play at all. It could be practise for hunting and fighting. Some dogs are hard-wired to find hunting, fighting, and killing very enjoyable activities. Once a dog is no longer a little puppy, the balance may change. The cat may not like playing anymore so it may run, which would, in turn, wind the dog up further. He could then chase and want to grab at the cat, and so the balance is lost.

Management

The best way to teach a dog to be fine around other animals is to prevent access to them so he can't go wrong. Have dog-free areas and cat-free areas in the house. Acclimatise the dog to the cat being there and teach him that the cat is boring. Always prevent chasing because the more fun a dog has chasing, the more difficult it will be for him to choose an alternative behaviour.

You shouldn't formally introduce them, and can't really expect them to get along happily, but you can teach them all to be okay about living under the same roof.

The answer really is to separate them. Playing with cats often ends in tears and vets' bills, even if your dog isn't a working terrier. Make sure the dog can't get to the cats. Make sure the cats can get away from the dog easily by installing baby gates and other barriers.

Teaching Tolerance

You can use *Click the Trigger* to teach an alternative behaviour to chasing. First, set up a situation where you are with the dog in one room and someone else oversees the cat in another room. There should be a baby gate in the doorway separating the rooms.

Sit with the dog on a lead and have your clicker (or marker word) and pot of yummy treats ready. Have the other person get the cat to walk past the baby gate. They could use a toy or smoked salmon lure, for instance. As soon as the dog sees the cat appear in the doorway, click and give him a treat. If he is too obsessed with the cat to take the food, then you either need a yummier (higher value) treat or you need to find somewhere where you can put a greater distance between the two animals. The treats stop as soon as the dog can no longer see the cat.

Continue over several sessions until the dog sees the cat and looks at you for a treat. The sessions should be just a few minutes long and end before everyone gets bored. The result will be a dog that likes the cat (sort of) because the cat predicts Good Things, so the dog should have no desire to chase the cat away. The dog will also have an alternative behaviour of looking at you and asking for a treat. Once the behaviour is learned, the clicker will no longer be needed, and the reward could change to a toy or lower value treats. You can then, for example, use part of the dog's daily food allowance as treats.

Give your Dog a Suitable Outlet for his Instincts

If your dog doesn't have an outlet for his sharp mind and his need to hunt or rag/shake his prey, he is likely to chase the cat more. Chasing and fighting with cats is a self-rewarding behaviour, no matter how badly he gets hurt, as he gets an adrenalin rush from it. It is therefore rewarding for him. To give him an outlet, you could:

- Buy or make toys such as flirt poles so your dog can chase and rag the toy on the end of the line
- Set up scent trails for him to track or things for him to sniff out and find
- Feed from food dispensing toys rather than a bowl

No Punishment

Do not punish your dog (even by shouting) for approaching or even chasing cats. If you do, he's likely to associate punishment with the cats rather than with his behaviour. Also, he's going to associate you with unpleasant things, which will reduce his desire to listen to you, work for you, and generally cooperate with you. By preventing a situation where you may be tempted to yell at your dog, it all gets a lot easier!

Remember

- Prevent the access to the cats by use of baby gates
- Teach an alternative behaviour using *Click the Trigger*
- Fill up his day with walks, clicker training, puzzle solving, eating from food dispensing toys and games that involve chasing, ragging, scenting, or digging
- No punishment

Chapter 11

Unwanted Behaviours

Undesirable Behaviours

By Abby Huxtable

For starters, most behaviours we class as undesirable or unwanted are totally natural to our dogs! They bark for communication, bounce when excited, have no hands and so need to use their mouths, and scavenge. However, human society perceives many of these as unwanted, so we want to change them.

We know how to prevent unwanted behaviours in the first place (see *Raising a Puppy*), but what do we do if our dogs form their own unwanted habits? Or come to us slightly later in their lives with unwanted behaviours already established?

This is where many may be tempted to use punishment or corrections. We *do not* advise either. Not only are punishment and corrections damaging to your relationship with your dog(s), but they are also incredibly hard to carry out effectively.

General consensus is that the timing of the reinforcement or punishment for a certain behaviour must be immediate for the dog to make the association with the behaviour he was performing. It's generally accepted that you have a maximum of one second to reinforce or punish behaviour. Any longer and the dog won't associate the consequence with the behaviour.

As we are human, we don't always get this timing spot on. We are often a bit slow! Therefore, if using punishment to try and erase a particular behaviour, you will often not get the timing right, and your dog won't make the connection that they are getting punished for that behaviour. This means they continue doing the behaviour and are getting punished, but they are not sure just what it is they are being punished for! Even though they are punishing the dog, the behaviour continues, so the human feels the need to escalate the punishment.

The dog is now getting punished more severely, but they don't know what for. They just know that the human punishes them. The relationship between the human and dog begins to break down, and the behaviour actually gets worse!

However, if we use positive reinforcement, our dog is getting rewarded even though our timing may be off. Statistics and probability tell us that if you repeat something often enough, you will eventually get it right. That means that our dogs are having fun with us, getting rewarded, and eventually, we will get the timing right often enough to make the behaviour stronger.

Another method people often suggest is ignoring the unwanted behaviour. The technical term for this is 'extinction', and although it does work, it is very hard to do!

The idea is that if you ignore the behaviour, it isn't being reinforced, and will therefore fade over time. However, a dog that is being ignored will usually escalate their behaviour by continuing for longer, vocalising louder, or jumping higher, for instance. This makes it much harder to ignore, so at some point we usually give in and react to them in some way, be it positive or negative. This will reinforce the escalated behaviour, as it has been rewarded! It is then even harder to ignore, as next time they will go straight to the escalation. This is frustrating for both us and our dogs.

We now know that neither punishment nor extinction are effective in getting rid of unwanted behaviours. They are extremely hard to carry out effectively, and can be damaging to our relationships with our dogs. So, what do we do instead?

The solution is to teach a mutually exclusive behaviour (MEB). This is also known as a differential reinforcement of an incompatible behaviour (DRI). This is basically an alternative behaviour that precludes the unwanted behaviour.

We can then reward the alternative behaviour, which then becomes the response to the stimulus instead of the undesired behaviour.

Note that if the unwanted behaviour is caused by fear, you would want to address the fear itself. An alternative behaviour would simply be another outlet for the fear, but your dog will still be experiencing the distress of that fear. See the chapter on: *Anxious and Fearful Dogs*.

Here are some examples of mutually exclusive behaviour:

- **Your dog jumps up at visitors**
  You have been shouting 'off' at them every time they do it. However, they are still practising the jump in the first place and often getting reinforced by the visitor greeting them anyway:
  - Have them on a lead to prevent the jump. As the visitor approaches, drop a few treats on the floor, or ask your dog for a sit or down. See also: *Four on the Floor – Preventing Jumping Up*.

- When they have four on the floor or their bottom down, the visitor then greets the dog in that position. You can also reward them if the visitor isn't going to greet your dog.
- They are getting reinforced for having all paws on the floor as they greeted the visitor, and so they learn to do that instead.

- **Rushing to the door when the doorbell rings**
  Teach them to go to their bed or place instead:

  - Record your doorbell sound. Play it and cue your dog to their bed or place.
  - Reward them when they have done so.
  - Repeat until they hear the doorbell and run to their bed or place.
  - Have a note on the door or disconnect your doorbell while you work on this to prevent them practising rushing to the door.

You can find some examples of mutually exclusive behaviour in *Four on the Floor – Preventing Jumping Up* and *Begging*. When it comes down to it, you just need to decide what you'd like your dog to do instead. You can then isolate the antecedent (the thing that causes the behaviour). Then practise and reinforce the new behaviour.

It works best if you can prevent them practising the old, unwanted behaviour while you strengthen the new behaviour. In effect, you do get extinction of the old behaviour, as they get reinforced for the new behaviour instead.

My Dog Doesn't Listen to Me
By Kay Bradnum

It's frustrating when you've worked hard with your dog, given him lots of love and all the right food, toys, and everything he needs – and you don't exist for him. It's even more frustrating when your Other Half just has to say the word and doggo is all ears and ready for instructions!

You'll often hear dog trainers and behaviourists talk about 'putting a value on' the word or action. This is the key to pretty much anything you want attention for. It just means to make it worth your dog's while to listen.

Let's look at some common situations in which your dog might not be paying you attention, and where you can fairly easily put a value on the desired behaviour. I'm going to assume you've already had a vet check and you know for sure there isn't a hearing problem.

- Your new puppy has arrived home! You've done everything by the book, but he doesn't respond to you at all; doesn't even seem to know his name. Well, why should he? It's still just a noise to him. If I stared at you and said, 'tractor, tractor, tractor', you'd think I was a bit bonkers and wonder if you should call someone. If I said 'tractor', and gave you £5 every time I said it, you'd pretty soon pay more attention, wouldn't you? Put value on his name. A tiny piece of sausage or cheese is £5 to a dog. A lovely game of tug is £5. An ear rub or back scratch is £5 for the right dog. Find out what floats his boat and use it!

- You've taught pup to sit; held a treat above his head until he sat, told him he's a good boy, and given him the treat. Now he won't do it without a treat over his nose. He just won't listen otherwise. You haven't put value on the cue 'sit'. You've bribed him and/or the treat has become a part of the cue. Look at other ways to get dog to sit or phase out the treats gradually and have them in a pot or pocket so they appear *after* the sit. Rather than luring, capturing a common behaviour is often the best way. Take a look at *Teaching a Down* for a good example. It puts value on the action itself before the cue is even added

- He's been such a good boy. He was very reliable and sensible for about six months, and now he's around a year old. What went wrong? Adolescence, that's what! Just go back several steps in your training, treat him like a much younger dog again, and when the hormones calm down, you'll come out the other side with the dog you had before. You must have put value on your cues before adolescence to have had such good results, so you'll get there again

- Your rescue dog has been an absolute dream for the first few weeks, but now he's ignoring you, being defiant, and doing as he pleases. Of course, he's actually not defiant. It's a sign that you're doing a good job of helping him reduce his stress levels, and he's coming out of a sort of 'shell shock' from the trauma of going into rescue, kennelling, fostering, and rehoming. He's ready to let you meet the dog he really is. The honeymoon period is over. Take it as a compliment, and get started on the real job of training – putting value on everything you ask of him

- Your dog behaves beautifully at training club, or at home, but you don't exist when you're at the dog park or out on a walk. The reason is two-fold:
  - Firstly, dogs don't generalise easily, so if you've taught a cue in the kitchen, teach it again in the front room, and the garden. And then just outside the gate. And anywhere else you can think of. It will get easier to teach each time. You will know when he understands that the cue applies everywhere.

- Secondly, it's much harder to concentrate somewhere exciting. You can't do your maths homework in Disneyland. I couldn't even recite my five times table on a roller coaster. Bear in mind your dog's age and limitations. Again, practise in as many places as you can think of. Make it easy for him to get it right, and he will slowly learn to concentrate everywhere. Or almost everywhere

• Your dog is a dream for one of you, but not the other. He listens to everything your partner says, but even though you do everything for him, he's not listening to you anymore. There could be lots of things at play with this one, so you'll need to do some analysing.

Does your partner have a deeper, stronger voice which the dog might find a little intimidating? That's not something you want to duplicate, but it is a cue for you both to rethink why your dog obeys. I'm sure neither of you meant to actually make him slightly afraid to disobey you.

Does your partner play a lot and have fun with him, while you do the feeding, grooming, and walking? Is it just food in a bowl, dog doesn't love the brush, and walking is a brisk 30 minutes because you have to go to work? You actually have three good opportunities to put value on yourself here. You could use some of each meal as training treats and do some fun stuff together. Work on gently desensitising to the brush and mix it up with something your dog enjoys doing. Even the walk can be more fun. Every now and again, bounce and squeak a bit, take a few running steps, and get your dog to nose-bump your fist, drop a few bits of kibble in the grass to show him your 'find'. Make sure you are worth listening to, just as your partner is.

This list isn't exhaustive, but it does cover the most common reasons that your dog might not be paying you attention. Hopefully, something will resonate with you, but if not, sit back and keep in mind that your dog isn't choosing to ignore you, he just hasn't been given a reason to pay attention. How can you put value on it?

Reacting to Kissing and Cuddling
by Sally Bradbury

Dogs don't do hugging, so when they see us doing it, they can find it difficult to understand. They will often see people cuddling and engaging in similar physical contact as conflict, so their reaction may be one of overarousal and joining in, or they may be worried by it.

With a little bit of time and training, it is easy to overcome your dog's negative reactions to you kissing a partner or hugging a child. For now, you will only hug without the dog in the room unless you are actively training him.

Here is how to change his mind from people hugging being a bad thing to it being a good thing.

- Use some delicious treats cut up into small pieces and sit together on the sofa or do whatever you would normally do. Touch each other on the shoulder briefly and give the dog a treat
- Repeat a few times
- Perhaps one of you then puts an arm around the other and treats the dog

I'll leave you to work out the various stages that you are going to go through, but it is important that you start at a level that does not get a reaction from your dog. Gradually do more each time, making sure that you keep him below his threshold until you can kiss and cuddle and smooch while your dog patiently waits for a treat.

This has got to be about the most fun you can have training a dog!

Things that Go Bump in the Night
Or why does my dog wake at an ungodly hour
By Sally Bradbury

Young puppies won't sleep all night unless you are very lucky, so expect to be up in the early hours with them needing the toilet. If puppy is happily sleeping with you, then there is a good chance that they will join you in a bit more sleep before their day needs to begin.

Given a stress-free introduction to sleeping through the night, most dogs will contentedly sleep the same hours as you. If you have an adult dog that wakes in the night or an hour before you want to get up and then wakes you, too, then here are some things you can try:

- Have the dog in the bedroom with you. This will be a good fix if the cause of waking is distress at being separated from you, or if the dog is being regularly disturbed in the room where he would usually sleep; wildlife in the back garden, a neighbour leaving to work an early shift, or the boiler switching on can all disturb a sleeping dog

- If your adult dog is still sleeping in a crate, then consider that he may prefer to be able to get up, stretch his legs, move somewhere else, and settle back to sleep. If he must be in a crate, address the reason why. Meanwhile, provide a larger crate with an area of warm bedding and an area where he can move away from it in case he is hot or cold
- If he is waking because he needs the toilet, make sure he is given the opportunity to completely empty before bedtime. Sometimes a short walk will get things moving. If he needs to poo early in the morning, then change the time of his last meal; usually to later so it doesn't need to exit until later in the morning
- If he's waking up hungry, then a supper time snack is the answer
- Finally, you can retrain his body clock by setting your alarm to just before he would normally wake so that you wake him up and then move it on by a minute a day until you are where you need to be. You may need to backtrack during this process

Oh, and don't expect a dog to know that he must sleep in on a weekend. If he does, that's a bonus.

Poo Eating (Coprophagia)
By Sally Bradbury

Poo eating, or coprophagia to use the scientific term, is normal. Undesirable, but nonetheless something that some dogs and many other species do.

There are various reasons why a dog may do this; learned from mum in the nest, hungry, undigested food present in the poo, habit, hiding the evidence if punished during toilet training, and many more.

Prevention is always the best policy. Pick up as soon as they go, especially if you have more than one dog. If it's other dog's poo, or the poo of any animal they are attracted to out and about, then a solid recall and a reliable 'leave' must be taught before letting your dog off lead.

If your dog is in the habit of watching your other dog(s) poo and diving for it, then the answer is to take them out separately for now. If he likes to poo and turn straight around to snack on it, then you can teach a positive interrupter. This is just a word or a noise that you pair with a high-value reward. It needs to be a happy sound so something like 'yay!', said in a cheery voice. Grab a few really yummy treats and with no distractions say 'yay!' and immediately give him a treat. Repeat this about ten times then wait for him to turn away from you, try the 'yay!' and he should turn to you for a treat. Then take him out on a lead and harness and as soon as he poos give him a 'yay!' as you gently move him away from the poo. Throw a few more treats on the ground for him so you can move in and remove the poo while he eats the treats. After a few sessions, he should reliably look to you for a treat after pooing and forget about snacking on the poo.

If you have a clicker trained dog, then the following method works well and has the added bonus of turning a poo eating dog into a poo finding dog:

1. Clear the yard/garden except for one poo
2. Have some very high-value treats, your clicker, and your dog
3. As soon as your dog looks at/sniffs the poo, click
4. If your dog is clicker savvy, they should turn to you for the treat and then spend the next ten minutes going through their repertoire trying to figure out what they did to get that click and treat
5. Then they'll give up and go back to their favourite pastime of eating poo. If the dog looks at the poo or their head goes down to, it click & treat

Depending on how good your timing is and how experienced your dog is, it should take between three and ten repetitions for the lightbulb moment; for the dog to 'get it' and know what they did to get the click & treat. Then you can put it on cue. 'Where's the poo?' Dog finds and looks at the poo, gets a click, leaves the poo, and comes to you for the treat.

This is useful when you are out with your dogs and one of them poos in the long grass some distance away. You can use your trained poo finding dog!

Frustrated Greeter

By Sally Bradbury

Does your dog dash up to other dogs in a rude manner and upset everyone at the park?

Enrol the help of any friends and family with dogs that he gets on with; ideally, dogs that are well-rounded and won't be intimidated by his lack of manners.

He doesn't need to practise his social skills on unknown dogs or dogs that you meet out and about. Besides, on lead meetings are not ideal because the lead will interfere with communication.

As with everything else, prevention is the first course of action. That means that when you are walking him, you need to give other dogs and people a wide berth. It might mean taking him somewhere in the car for a walk.

Then you need to find somewhere where you can watch dogs and people passing in the distance and where you can teach him an alternative response to seeing them.

If you clicker train, you can use a method called *Click the Trigger*. You can use a marker word, such as 'yes' instead of using a clicker.

Every time he sees a dog, you click and give him a treat. You should be far enough away from the trigger for him to want the reward rather than fixate on the other dog.

So, lots of practise in different places, with him seeing a dog in the distance and getting a click and treat. After a while, he will look or may even pretend to look, and look back to you quickly in anticipation of the reward. Then you have Stage Two; see a dog, turn back to you to tell you he has seen it, click and treat. Continue in this fashion. Vary the criteria, for example closer to the trigger or with you walking, but not towards other dogs until you are both really competent.

Once you have him ignoring other dogs for the most part, then you can also use play with other dogs as a reward for not rushing at them.

Arrange to meet one of your volunteers with their dog; you will need to have them appear at a strategic point. Have your dog on his long trailing line. When he sees the dog, stand on his line and the other dog will stop approaching as pre-arranged. Call him back to you or wait for the auto check in. He can choose to stay where he is and look at the dog in the distance, or come back to you and be released to go and play. It will take a few repetitions for him to learn how to earn the reward that he wants. You will need several sessions with several different dogs, and you will also need to vary the rewards. He doesn't always get to go and play because it won't always be appropriate. Sometimes he gets food, sometimes a game with you.

Your aim is for him to see a dog and return to you when off lead. This gives you time to ascertain whether it would be appropriate to allow him to go and see the dog.

Jumping in Excitement at Visitors
By Sally Bradbury

If your dog leaps excitedly at everyone who walks through the door, then there are various things you can do.

You could put your dog behind a stair gate. If necessary, place one above another so he can't jump or climb over. Then you can choose to reward any behaviour that is in the right direction, for example front feet on the floor. You can either give food rewards or allow the visitor to fuss him through the gate in a way that keeps the front feet on the floor.

You could also have him on a lead and harness and hold him away from the door. Then have the visitor come in and stand still while you reward the behaviour you want. The visitor moves forward but steps back if he starts to jump.

You could have your dog on lead or behind the gate and invite ten friends for a coffee morning. They get coffee and chocolate cake as a reward for helping you train the dog. They would come in the front door and go out the back door at one-minute intervals without acknowledging the dog. The same people coming and going would eventually become boring and then the dog can learn how to earn rewards by not jumping.

See also: *Four on the Floor – Preventing Jumping Up.*

Counter Surfing

By Sally Bradbury

You can either keep surfaces clear of food or the dog out of the kitchen to prevent the dog from learning to counter surf. Don't forget that any behaviour that is rewarded is likely to be repeated. For the dog that has already learned to counter surf, teach an alternative behaviour.

Take a chopping board, a knife, and tin of hot dog sausages. Open the tin, tip any brine down the sink, and rinse the sausages. Take out a sausage and spend some time carefully cutting it into small pieces.

Now, just turn sideways and block his view of the chopping board. If he has all four feet on the floor, toss him a bit of sausage. If he is barking, whinging, or whining, then ignore him and continue to chop up sausage. If he stops, chuck him a bit of sausage.

Give him maybe half a dozen rewards for having four feet on the floor and being quiet. Be aware that you are neither asking him to do anything, nor are you asking him to stop doing anything. All you need say to him is a quiet 'good boy' when you reward him.

Now, hold off on the next reward and see if he offers anything even better. It could be to move away from the worktop. He might offer a sit or a down, if either of those has a history of reward. Basically, reward the behaviour that you like. The more repetitions you do, the more he is learning what pays off. As a result, when you are preparing food, those are the behaviours that he will offer. You will occasionally still need to reinforce them once learnt.

Door Dashing

By Sally Bradbury

If you have a dog that dashes through doors at every opportunity, especially exterior doors, **always** put him on a lead before opening the door. At other times, keep two doors or baby gates between him and outdoors.

See also: *Living in a Multi-Dog Household, Going through doors and gates*

Chasing and Lunging at Cars
By Sally Bradbury

If your dog is reactive to cars and other traffic, you need to start off by staying away from roads. Go for walks in areas with little or no traffic, even if this means driving somewhere for exercise. This ensures that he isn't practising the behaviour.

I recommend that you introduce your dog to clicker training. You can just use a marker word instead, but it's quicker with a clicker.

Follow exactly the same protocol as detailed in *Reasons for Excessive Barking, For Alert Barking*.

Begging
By Sally Bradbury

If your dog begs for food during meals, the solution is to teach an alternative behaviour. To start with, don't eat in front of the dog. You may have to eat meals in shifts, with someone entertaining the dog while the other person eats.

Then at a quiet time, begin to teach a more desirable behaviour. Sit at the table with a cuppa, a biscuit, and some treats for the dog. Decide what you would like him to do; should he lie under the table, go to his bed, or do something else? Toss a treat under the table/on his bed. Do this a few times. He may then try and get you to give him another. Continue to drink your coffee and say nothing at all. Don't be tempted to tell him what to do or what not to do. If it his choice to do it, it will be a more reliable behaviour.

Now, wait for any behaviour or movement that is in the right direction. Looking away would suffice for starters. Reward every behaviour that is not begging, gradually shaping the behaviour until you get to where you want to be.

You will need a lot of sessions, gradually increasing the difficulty, before he is ready to show off his new skill at mealtimes.

Digging
By Sally Bradbury

Digging is a natural behaviour for a dog. Most dogs dig. If all her needs are being met, then just provide her with a digging pit. This could be the corner of a flower bed or a child's sandpit. Let her watch you bury some treasure there, like a bone, a toy, or a biscuit. Then help her dig it up. Do this a few times, then bury the treasure when she isn't watching and let her discover it. If you continue to occasionally bury something for her, she will soon only dig where you want her to.

Shadow or Light Chasing

Chasing shadows or lights can start as a momentary distraction, which the owner finds amusing, but can soon escalate to a severe behavioural problem. The behaviour may have a serious and negative impact on the dog's quality of life.

The chase is the start of the predatory sequence, which is natural to many dogs, but as there is no way to complete the sequence, it's incredibly frustrating for the dog; it can become an obsession, as the dog attempts to catch his 'prey'. This is the reason why laser toys should never be used with a dog.

Prevent the behaviour as much as possible by closing curtains to prevent shadows, covering anything shiny to prevent reflections, and walking when the sky is overcast. In the early stages, you should be able to distract your dog and guide him to a more appropriate behaviour, but in the later stages you are likely to need expert help from a veterinary behaviourist.

Chapter 12

Skills for a Happy Life

Where do I Start? What Should my Dog Know?
The important stuff with a new dog
By Kay Bradnum

Does your dog know that he's in his forever home? Safe and loved? That you will always have his back and protect him from things he's afraid of? Then you've already done the important stuff.

When they first bring home their new puppy or rescue, many people feel absolutely overwhelmed with how much there is to do, how much there is to teach, and where on earth they should start! Many sources suggest starting with things like sit, stand, down, come, and stay. We say there's a much earlier starting point, and it has nothing to do with teaching tricks on cue.

Every dog should be with someone they can trust. Your dog needs to learn that you will provide food and shelter, you won't push him into situations he can't cope with until he's ready, and if you get it wrong and he does end up in such a situation, you certainly won't tell him off for not coping. He needs to learn the world is a safe and fun place to be, that he can always tell you when something worries him, and that you will help him. It will help him to learn that he's safe and loved in the family and that you will always be there for him. It helps you, and his confidence, if he knows where the toilet is.

That's it. Everything else is the icing on the cake.

After that, think about what's really important to you. Think about the so-called 'basics' above:

- **Sit.** Does your dog really need to sit? What will happen if he doesn't learn to do it on cue? Many deep-chested muscular dogs, such as the greyhound and the Doberman, find sitting very uncomfortable. All young puppies and many giant breeds, like the St Bernard, can find it an effort to use those muscles. If your dog sits happily, you can add in a cue when they sit naturally so they learn to do it when asked. However, as long as he will stay quietly by your side when needed, a sit isn't really necessary
- **Stand.** This can be useful, but it isn't a big deal. You can easily give treats and put the behaviour on cue when your dog happens to stand anyway
- **Down.** See: *Stand*

- **Stay.** You will need to teach your dog how to cope when alone, but stay while you walk ten paces away and back again? OK, you'll need this if you want to compete in dog sports such as agility or obedience. If you don't, what is it good for? You're never going to leave your dog like that. He's always going to be on a lead if it's not safe for him to move

- **Come (Recall).** Yes, this one is important if your friend is to enjoy time off lead, but it doesn't have to be taught in the first few weeks. A really reliable recall, which works in in almost every situation, will take up to two years to perfect. Don't rush!

Remember that all dogs are learning 24/7, not just when you have a training session.

That's not to say you shouldn't teach all of these. Teaching and learning exercises can be a fantastic way to bond with your dog, especially if it's all done through play and at your dog's pace. We're just saying that you don't need to get hung up on the fact that the lady down the road has taught her 14-week-old collie to competitive obedience standard, and feel you have to do the same.

There are many different types of dog sports you can try. As well as obedience, there's agility, flyball, treibball, mantrailing, canicross, herding, heelwork to music (HTM), Schutzhund (IGP), bikejoring, trick training, carting, mushing, and lure-coursing, to name just a few. If you and your dog want to give it a go, then do it and have fun! But if your thing is a long sniffari going nowhere, that's a great thing to do, too. In fact, all dogs should have sniffaris as well as anything else they do. But sports and tricks generally? They aren't essential.

When it comes down to it, if your dog knows that he's in his forever home, safe and loved, and that you will always have his back, then you've already done the important stuff!

Exercising Your Dog's Mind

By Kay Bradnum

We all know to take care of our dog's physical exercise and, for most, a couple of good walks a day make the difference between a hyper, almost out-of-control dog, and one who's content to snooze by the fire in the evening.

However, there are lots of times when walks aren't the answer; they're not for dogs on restricted exercise, or when you can't walk because of extreme weather conditions, nor are they for dogs who are just too fearful or anxious to cope with a walk. Very fearful dogs might need to be left in peace altogether for several days, weeks, or longer. If your dog is happy with you at home but afraid of walks, no walk at all is the best thing. We can just tire their brain instead. Twenty minutes of hard thinking can equal a good hour's walk. Think how tired you are if you've spent all day swotting for an exam or writing up a difficult presentation.

A few simple training tasks might be all you need. Teach a 'high five', 'roll over', 'play dead', 'say your prayers', and so on. Teach your dog to touch your hand whenever you hold it out. Teach him the names of his toys or to put them away. It doesn't have to be anything formal or 'special', just as long as it's fun for both of you.

There are many food enrichment toys on the market; lickimats and Kongs are the ones most people know. These are great, but there are lots of free alternatives to food toys:

- Teach him the Cups Game. Put one treat under a cup and encourage him to touch it with his nose or paw to get the treat. Once he's understood that, add another cup. Once he is choosing the correct cup each time, move them around, then add a third. It's fun for both of you
- Instead of giving him his food in a bowl, throw it on the grass for him to forage for it. This is otherwise known as scatter feeding
- When you have time, lay short trails of food for him to follow
- Play hide and seek. The hider should have a toy to play with the dog when found
- Hide a treat in a cardboard toilet or kitchen roll tube and fold the ends over for him to open
- Put a few treats in a cardboard box with some scrunched up newspaper and let him find them.
- If he's fed kibble, spread it on an old dog towel, and roll it up for him to search for. When he gets good at this, cut the leg off an old pair of jeans and roll that up with kibble hidden in each layer
- Put some treats in an old plastic bottle with no lid. Let him play with the bottle to get them out. If he struggles, poke a few holes in it. Before you start, make sure that the noise doesn't frighten him

Scent work is also a good activity for tiring your dog.

Teaching Self-Control
By Sally Bradbury

Self-control is defined as the ability to manage emotions, impulses, and behaviour, and to resist temptation. It is an inhibitory control, which is part of a set of cognitive skills known as executive function. This is necessary to be able follow directions, maintain focus, regulate emotions, and attain goals.

Using Food

Have a treat that your dog wants in a closed hand. Allow him to sniff your hand. He may lick or nibble. If you are in danger of losing your hand, then start this exercise with a toy. When he backs off, however briefly, open your hand and give him the treat. Repeat until he understands to wait to be given the treat. Use a release word such as 'take it' or 'yes'.

Don't say 'wait', or anything at all; particularly avoid saying 'no' or 'ah ah'. That isn't *self*-control.

Next step, show him a treat in an open hand and use the release cue for him to take it. Increase the time between showing the hand and giving the release word. If he moves to take it before the release, close your hand.

Variations on this include food on the floor, food on paws (if he isn't sensitive about feet being touched), food dropped, food thrown, and not being released to get the food, but being called away for a better treat. Be sure to practise in different locations.

Using a Toy

You need your dog to be focussed on the toy.

Decide on your release word. Let's use 'yes'. Roll the toy away and say 'yes' at the same time. Repeat several times.

Next, with a finger in his collar or holding his harness, roll the toy away. Wait for the slightest backward movement or pause from him while looking at the toy. Say 'yes' and let him go to the toy. Repeat this, increasing the time between pause and release by a fraction of a second each time.

Aim for a two to five second pause without needing to hold his harness or collar. No need to ask for a wait. The dog is choosing to wait for the release, otherwise it isn't self-control.

Now gradually add variations one at a time.

Throw the toy, place the toy, roll the toy away, use different toys.

Crouch down next to him, stand next to him, change sides, move away after throwing the toy, move away before throwing the toy (for this last one, you may add the wait cue).

Finally, vary the locations.

Doors and Gates

Teach your dog a default wait at doors and gates, so that he waits before being released, without being asked.
See: *Living in a Multi-Dog Household, Going through doors and gates*

Teaching a Down
By Sally Bradbury

Take your dog to the 'smallest room' in the house (bathroom). Make sure you have a pot of small and tasty treats, a good book, and a coffee or whatever you drink.

Close the door and sit on the seat that is conveniently provided in there.

Have a treat concealed in your hand.

Read your book but keep one eye on puppy. When she lays down, toss her the treat so she has to get up to get it. Go back to your book, wait for her to lie down again, and repeat. You say nothing except for a quiet 'good' as she lies down.

Continue in this way over several sessions. When she knows that lying down gets her a treat, and you'll know when she knows, then you add the word that you are going to use. You say 'flat', 'down', 'lie down', whatever works for you. She lies down and gets a treat. Now try it in other places, but start back at the beginning again with no cue yet. She'll get it really quickly the next time.

Next, give the reward to the dog while she is still lying down, so she doesn't need to get up. This ensures she is being reinforced while she is performing the behaviour and will enable you to build duration. Then add in a release cue, such as 'break', and reward the dog for responding to the release. Down = reward in place. Break = reward for moving. This ensures that the dog remains in the down until being released.

174

Teaching a Down at a Distance

Once your dog is reliably responding to the cues, move to an outdoor environment with plenty of space. Use either food or a toy that you can throw as a reward. Cue the down when your dog is a short distance from you. Reward success while your dog is lying down. Release and toss the reward away from your dog. If you have a dog that loves to chase a toy and anticipates that you'll throw it, this is by far the easiest way to get a down at a distance. Start to throw, cue the down as the dog moves away from you, cue the release and throw the toy.

Desensitising to Car Journeys

By Vidhyalakshmi Karthikeyan

The first thing to to consider when your dog is afraid of riding in the car is whether she is experiencing car sickness. For this, you need to speak to your vet as there are medications that can be prescribed to reduce motion sickness. If she is feeling sick, it's going to be hard to change her emotions about the car until that has been managed.

Assuming that your dog doesn't suffer from motion sickness (or, if she does, that it has been addressed by a vet), then here's what you would do:

- First, find the distance from the car at which she is aware of the car trip, but not showing any fearful behaviour. Think alert but not afraid. This is the distance where you start training
- Every day, place a portion of her meals (or some small treats) in a big pouch. Sit in the car with the engine off, the door open, and even your legs facing the outside touching the ground, but no plans to go anywhere whatsoever
- Have her on a harness and as long a line as you can get. This is just for safety. If the area where your car is parked is secure, then she can be off lead if preferred
- Then toss each piece of her food just behind her, one at a time, so she increases space between herself and the car to get it. This relieves any pressure on her to get closer to the car
- Do not lure her to the car. She must take every step to the car by herself, of her own volition
- Eventually, she'll be close enough to the car to get in. Do the same for jumping in. Give her a ramp if that's helpful
- When she's at the stage where she's sitting in the car, which will be far down the line, do some other training with her in the car

- Feed meals in the car. Make sure that everything nice happens in the back seat, or wherever you want her to settle
- The next step is to have the engine on, but don't drive anywhere yet. Rinse and repeat
- Put into gear, let the tyres roll forward half a metre. Rinse and repeat. This part might also take a while.

You'll be spending a lot of time around the car without moving an inch. So, make sure you don't force her to get into the car and drive with you until she's ready. That's going to mean staying within walking distance of your home, if you're not already.

Road to Nowhere

By Jo Maisey

Your dog may get overexcited by car journeys because they predict a fabulous event, such as a good walk. This could result in her vocalising by barking or whining; sometimes for the whole journey, or sometimes just as you arrive at your destination. Identify the triggers that set your dog off yelling. For mine, these were parking up, turning off the engine, and unclipping the seatbelt. Depending on the trigger, these are the steps you can take to alleviate this issue:

- Get in the car with your dog
- Just sit in the driver's seat with the engine off and read for a while
- Get out of the car and take the dog out too. Go back indoors
- Repeat until there is no vocalising
- Progress to sitting in the car and reading a book, but now with the engine running
- Repeat until there is no vocalising
- Progress to just driving around the block and straight back home again
- Repeat until there is no vocalising
- Progress to driving somewhere that is *not* your usual dog walking spot, park the car, stay in the car for a while with your dog (you can read your book), then turn around and go home again
- Repeat until there is no vocalising
- Progress to driving to your usual dog walking spot, park up, read a book, your dog stays in the car, then turn around and go home again
- Repeat until there is no vocalising
- If your dog is triggered by things such as turning off the engine, or perhaps unclipping the seatbelt, add those steps in as appropriate

The aim is for car journeys to not *always* predict something exciting, but to become boring so your dog learns to relax. You can carry out each step a few times a day. The process can take several days or weeks. It would be best not to drive your dog for a walk while you follow this process. Wait until the vocalising has stopped. Even then, it would be wise to re-visit the process now and again, so that the car does come to predict only exciting things once more.

Moving To a New House
By Rebecca Köhnke

In my experience, dogs cope amazingly well with change as long as they're with someone they trust.

Whenever we moved with the dogs, we tried to:

- Pack up gradually *or* have movers do the packing while the dogs were out to avoid a few chaotic days
- Leave their stuff in its usual place and their routine as unchanged as possible
- Take them to the new area for walks several times ahead of the move, so the area became somewhat familiar
- Get them out of the house for the actual furniture moving process. We either left them in the care of a trusted person or took them for a long walk. The first time we moved, we didn't do this and our completely chilled and confident pup nearly had a breakdown when they took his sofa
- Take their stuff with us, so that when the dogs arrived, I could go in and prepare their most important areas before they came in
- Organise to have an Adaptil or Pet Remedy diffuser set up in both the old and new place a week or two before the move. That way, both homes had a similar, familiar, and calming scent
- Arrange all or some of the furniture in a familiar pattern

I wouldn't get the pup a new bed to celebrate the move, or anything like that. I'd make sure that as much furniture as possible is familiar, paying particular attention to his safe and comfortable places. You can replace with new things later, of course, once you're all settled.

Keep in mind that you may need to refresh on toilet training, because dogs don't generalise well to other houses. They need to learn where the external doors are first.

Also, keep in mind that a new environment can trigger some separation anxiety, so try to take some time off to settle in with them. Gradually see how they feel about being left.
See: *Chapter 3 Separation Anxiety or Frustration.*

Remember to look into potential dog sitters or walkers in the new area ahead of time and introduce before the move if you can.

Muzzle Love
By Abby Huxtable

Muzzles are an absolutely fantastic tool. They also have a big stigma attached to them. Everyone assumes a muzzled dog is aggressive. Fortunately, with the increase in more positively educated trainers and owners following suit, this opinion is slowly changing.

Muzzles are used for a huge range of reasons; yes, a dog may be scared and so have a bite history, but they may have been attacked and be worried by other dogs, they may be a rescue who is terrified of people, they may love eating yukky things that make them poorly, or they may be hunting dogs who we are protecting the wildlife from.

Muzzles also have the added benefit of making people more wary of our dogs, so they enable us to safely work with our dogs with less risk from the 'oh, it's fine, he's friendly' brigade, or random people and children touching our dogs without permission.

Just as with any of our tools – leads, harnesses, grooming equipment – we do need to carefully introduce muzzles to our dogs to ensure they are happy and confident wearing them.

Also, like any of our tools, the muzzle is not a solution to a behavioural issue. You still need to work on the behaviour itself; same as a lead and harness is not a solution for pulling on the lead, you still need to teach your dog loose lead walking. A muzzle will not make your dog feel happy around strange people, you still need counter-conditioning to strange people. Your muzzle can just help gain more space when around people and prevent an accident happening.

It is a good idea to teach all of our dogs to wear a muzzle, as you never know when we might need to help them out. They may have a painful injury that needs attending by the vet or they may have a nasty knot in their coat that the groomer needs to remove. They may be competing in dog sports that require muzzles, such as lure coursing, or even dog sports, where there are a large number of dogs and they need that bit of space.

Muzzle training, just like any husbandry training, is always a great idea and can be a fun game to play on an evening when you want to channel your dog's focus!

We would always recommend a basket style muzzle, so they are able to eat, drink and pant while wearing it. It is also really important that a muzzle is correctly fitted, so it is secure and comfortable on your dog. There are muzzles in all shapes, colours and sizes, and many companies make custom fit muzzles, so you can buy one specifically for your own dog.

Printed in Great Britain
by Amazon

30163924R00106